PEOPLE SKILLS

For Tough Times

The Keys to Getting Along

Camaron J. Thomas, Ph.D.

The Troy Book Makers
www.thetroybookmakers.com

To Steve,

You Were a Hero for Us All,

And West

Acknowledgements

Everyone will have an opinion about this book. Some will say it's not scholarly enough or too hands-on for the professional problem-solver. Others will say it's too spiritual or not spiritual enough. Regardless, it would not be half the book it is, were it not for the couples, families, and many groups who have allowed me into their private moments over the years as their mediator. It still takes a special person to try mediation. I have been given this privilege by many people whose stories and experiences helped shape the composite cases contained in this book. For this, I am deeply appreciative: without each and every one of you, this book would simply not be possible.

I also want to thank my many teachers who, in different settings – from government to technology to Ayurveda to Yoga to private business to mediation – have helped guide my studies and develop my thinking. There have been many friends, as well, who have read and re-read this text, commented and critiqued it, without complaint. The love and dedication of Roseann Figliomeni has been a special source of strength, especially when things seemed bleak. And the unending talent, commitment, and dedication of John Durnin also deserves special note; every time I faltered, you were there. I am forever in your debt. And finally, yet never last, I need to thank the girls who have sat by me, faithfully, patiently, dreaming their puppy dreams...and my husband who not only helped create this book, he helped create my life; no acknowledgement could ever go far enough.

Table of Contents

Introduction 1

SECTION ONE: CHANGING YOUR LIFE

1. The Basic Tools for Getting Along 17
   Why Conversation Matters • So It Goes • Positional
   Bargaining • Some Life Changing Tools

2. More than Tools 31
   It's a Tough World Out There • Interests-Based
   Negotiations • Other Ways to Deal with Differences •
   A Fresh Look • An Area for Further Exploration

SECTION TWO: CHANGING YOUR MIND

3. The Source of Conflict... 45
   When Good Goes Bad • Self Proving • A Self to Defend
   • Becoming Somebody • The Mind Contracts • The First
   Mental Lock • Threatened and Re-Active • At the Zoo •
   An Area for Further Exploration

4. A Change of Mind.. 59
   The Physical Side of the Equation • How to Stop Self
   Proving • More Than Self Awareness • Taking Time
   to Notice • Awareness Comes • The Key • An Area for
   Further Exploration

SECTION THREE: CHANGING YOUR RELATIONSHIPS

5. Relating to Others...73
   Born to Read People • Framing the Experience • The
   Second Mental Lock • How "We Assume We Know" •
   You Need to... • An Area for Further Exploration

6. Being with "Family"...86
   The Dance of Conflict • The Emotions We Feel •
   Beginning to Hear • Feeling Heard • Not Active
   Listening • Reflect First • The Key • An Area for Further
   Exploration

7. A New Definition of Help.....................................98
   The Will – Take 1 • What's Said and Left Unsaid •
   The Will – Take 2 • The Will – Take 3 • Crystallized
   Reflection • A Different Kind of Knowing • An Area for
   Further Exploration

8. Working with Others..113
   Different and Yet... • Just Like Family • What We Bring
   to Work • Climbing Out • Making it Work • Being
   Present at Work • Choosing the Relationship • An Area
   for Further Exploration

SECTION FOUR: CHANGING THE WORLD

9. When Doing the Right Thing Isn't 133
   A Social Identity • The Third Mental Lock • How We
   Prove "There's One Right Way" • When Hate is Part of
   Conflict • In Search of Something Solid • A National
   Mind Rut • An Area for Further Exploration

Chapter 10. The Other Choice 144
    Pain and More Pain • This One I Simply Cannot Buy
    • The Third Option • Ask a Good Question and Make
    a Request • A Transpersonal Approach to Conflict •
    Iterative Decisions • The Final Key • A Transpersonal
    Approach to Dealing with Differences

Biblography 159

Introduction

This is a book about changing how we talk with one another; specifically, about how we deal with differences. It's a book about people skills – the skills we all think we have.

Talk, Talk, Talk, Talk, Talk, Talk, Talk

Most of us assume we know how to talk with another person. Every human resource director is convinced he's a good mediator; every manager believes she's a natural problem solver; every salesperson is sure he can read people; every doctor is confident of her bedside manner. Ask any wife and she will tell you what her husband just said, or meant to say; ask any husband and he will tell you precisely what happened to cause the argument. Yet despite all this certainty, we often don't get along – there's a lot of talk, but very little *connection*.

In fact, with the proliferation of the cell phone, we talk *all* the time. We "talk at", "talk around", "talk over", even "talk to", but we seldom "talk with." Listen-in to one side of the pressing matter unfolding in the snack-food isle or the heated debate transpiring in the parking lot, and you're quickly reminded of how little we talk *with* one another. While we like to think of ourselves as good listeners, strong communicators, and avid problem-solvers, we each know a boss who can't give clear instructions, a parent who can't listen long enough to hear, a person who struggles to voice her opinion and one who'd rather yell than even try. We end up in touch but uninvolved; in contact but not actually engaged with another person.

When we think of listening, talking, and problem-solving, we often assume these skills are naturally endowed. If the level of hostility in the world is any indication, this is certainly not the case. Think back to the last few conversations you've had. How often did you really get your message across? How often did you feel understood and intimately hear the other person? How often did you move beyond all that and connect on a broader, more workable plane?

Problem-*Solving?*

It's easy to confuse the process of problem-solving with the product of problem-solving. Human beings, as a group, are addicted to "figuring things out." We love to study what went wrong, figure out who is to blame/who's at fault/who started it, and decide on the best course of action. But figuring things out is not the same as solving the problem. Most of our "figuring" takes place inside our heads: we get one, maybe two, perspectives and then rush to a "solution." In our personal lives, this creates more gossip and commiserating than real problem-solving. On a larger scale, it produces a lot of rules, policies, and otherwise good ideas that solve the wrong problem, if they work at all.

Far fewer of us want to actually engage in the dialogue that needs to happen to hear a problem and then try to solve it. We don't want to face the hurt feelings, the sometimes harsh words, loud voices, allegations and accusations that can accompany differences, arguments, and conflict. Besides, we've learned from experience that resolving conflict can be painful long after the problem goes away; that our so-called solutions rarely resolve the underlying issues which only resurface in time; and try as we may, our relationships always suffer. It's hard to stay friends, co-workers, partners, or even close, after a serious misunderstanding.

So what do *you* do when you're confronted with differences? When your best friend tells you that you're selfish? Or a colleague fires off a department-wide memo criticizing your hiring practices as sexist? Or your "ex" claims you're a dead-beat-Dad who's never been there for your daughter? Or your sister refuses to tell your Mom she can't drive anymore? Or your spouse begs, for the ten-thousandth time, "Why don't you just talk to me?" What do you do when the contractor walks out on an obviously sloppy job? Or your son snaps that he's trying to clean the garage, if you'd just stop controlling his every move? Or your boss gives the cushy assignment to another staffer because "you're obviously in over your head"? Or your neighbor's summer parties are getting altogether out of hand? What do you do when you're angry, embarrassed and resentful, insulted, and surprised, all at the same time?

Differences are Scary

As a student of conflict and a mediator, one thing I've learned is that differences should be expected. In fact, if you're not experiencing them, you're probably not living fully. With so many people living on a finite planet and so much to be done, it's only natural to find differences. Differences should be anticipated – they're a natural part of being with others, residing in a community, and being alive.

But few of us have an elaborate repertoire for dealing with differences. Rather, we expect people to agree with us and when they don't, we feel threatened. We lunge at the conversation with something to prove. We rely on a narrow, time-worn set of reactions we hope will prove our point, defend our position, or make the problem go away. In a flash, the discussion escalates into an argument where it suddenly becomes absolutely necessary to convince the other person we're right; or minimally, walk away with our honor intact. *It can feel like a life or death situation.*

And conflict can happen over the stupidest things:
Wife: "Did the recycling bins blow away?"
Husband: "Yeah."
Wife: "Oh crap," starting to fret, "I don't know where

3

we go to replace those. The one was owned by the garbage collection company."

Husband: "I got them, relax. We don't need to replace them. You always get so wired about this stuff. Just chill out. It's a recycling bin, for God's sake. What are you going to do when it's something really important?"

Under the right conditions, this minor exchange could trigger a week-long siege. If it's been a hard day for either of them, or this is a well-worn argument about her getting worked up over things, or the wife has always questioned her husband's commitment to conservation and this proves her point, what began as a simple discussion in the kitchen could mushroom into a full scale altercation. It might be the last straw in a marriage gasping for breath; another example of irreconcilable differences in the final court papers.

Too often we mistake the feeling of not being understood for something else. We decide the relationship isn't working or we've fallen out of love; that we're not getting the respect we deserve, not cared about or valued. Too often we leave a good place to work, a relationship, a friend, a family, just because we can't deal with differences. Usually, we leave too soon.

Individuals, Groups, and Nations

We're especially vulnerable to react poorly when things really matter. At some level, this seems odd. In the face of differences over an important issue, it would make sense to anticipate objections, weigh our words carefully, make our points deliberately, and come prepared with options. But in conflict, rationale and logic seldom prevail. Take the Father who strolls in forty minutes late for a custody mediation and leads off with, "I'm here to get the kids to come and live with me. You've already shown you're not fit and the court knows it. So, are you ready to deal or what?" When the Mother storms out in a huff and taunts, "See you in court, you bastard," the Father's likely to believe she's just proven his point and say, "See, there's no working with her." The conversation dead-ends before it begins.

We handle conflict in a group setting, and even on the world stage, in very much the same way. Consider the following controversies:

- A local firm decides to move its neighborhood, home-town office to a new, state-of-the-art facility, outside of town with limited parking;
- The school board wants to close its "homey" elementary school and merge it into the middle school complex;
- A powerful development company elects to put up 5,000 new homes on some of the last remaining green space in the community;
- The wind turbines being erected to generate cheap electricity risk ruining the perfect view of the landscape; and/or,
- A nation's ships drift, perhaps mistakenly, into the waters of a sovereign country.

We attack these issues with the same fervor, outrage, and animosity as the problems we face at home. The results are likely to be just as contested, divisive, and emotional. And with more people involved, these larger conflicts generate more reactivity, more posturing, and, on balance, a higher volume of bravado. Even in a strictly business deal, when the moves and counter-moves are plotted and planned in advance, it's easy to come unglued. If someone backs out of the deal, offends us in front of our superiors, or infers that we're not trustworthy, we feel threatened and react. Chances are we end up inserting and asserting ourselves all over the place. As we've said, it can feel like a life or death situation.

In sum, regardless of the nature of the issue or its scale, most of us don't handle differences well. We dodge the problem as long as we can, deal with it in subtle and not-so-subtle ways and then, we call a lawyer. The net result is often a total communication breakdown. And then we move onto the next problem.

Working with Conflict

When we confront differences, most of us begin with informal measures to try to resolve the problem – we try to "negotiate" or bargain with the person or group. If this fails and the issue is important enough, we progress towards litigation. Yet there are many ways to handle conflict. In fact, there's an entire field devoted to alternative ways to manage conflict.

According to the Association for Conflict Resolution, alternatives to judicial intervention include mediation, arbitration, dispute management, negotiation, and collaborative law (See ACR Web Site). Mediation in particular, involves the assistance of an outside third party to help settle problems. This person or persons may be a professional mediator, a council of elders, one's parents or an extended family member, a board of directors, a religious or political leader, an executive designee or group such as an in-house mediation unit, or a high ranking official charged with dispute resolution. Other means of redress include legislative and extra-legal approaches such as sit-ins or fasting and, of course, violence in its numerous forms.

Mediation has been around since the beginning of time and been present in some form in nearly every culture on the planet (See Moore, 2003). It was first brought to the United States predominately by the Puritans and Quakers who wanted a more informal way to resolve disputes and handle differences. While mediation initially focused on labor relations, it was later used to handle civic concerns such as urban violence and as an adjunct to the judicial system. Since that time, mediation has extended its reach into the armed forces, commercial dealings, the postal service, consumer rights, crisis intervention; fields such as education, health care, public policy and regulations, the environment, and criminal justice; and arenas such as international law, housing, family disputes, divorce, adoption, and elder care.

Not surprisingly, along with this growth, there have been many excellent books written on the subject. Beginning in the early eighties and most notably with <u>Getting to Yes</u> (1981) by Fisher and Ury, these books helped attract a great deal of attention to the field. More recently, texts have focused on honing the skills of professional problem-solvers and increasingly, those of the lay-person. These books generally fall into three categories.

The first concentrates on the tools of mediation. Texts such as <u>Crucial Confrontations</u> (Patterson, Grenny, McMillan, and Switzler, 2005) and <u>Everyday Negotiations</u> (Kolb, Ph.D., and Williams, Ph.D., 2003) are largely "how-to" books. These books provide the reader with techniques to solve the right problem, set the proper environment, map the conflict, shape the conversation, generate multiple solutions, and analyze choices. They help parties identify areas of mutual intent and common interests, get and keep the conversation going, use incentives and pressure, and control the process of negotiation in order to nail down a solution. How-to books often include specific tools. In <u>Beyond Machiavelli,</u> for example, authors provide tools such as the "Four Quadrant Analysis" and the "Seven Elements of a Conflict Situation", to help problem-solvers organize their thinking, analyze and diagnose barriers to progress, flesh out choices, and generate fresh ideas (Fisher, Kopelman, and Schneider, 1996).

Books in the second category take a more psychological, inward-looking approach to conflict resolution; almost self-counseling in nature. They seek to solve "the anger behind the argument", suggesting that since we can only change ourselves, we need to analyze the thoughts and behavior around how we deal with conflict. Books such as <u>We Can Work It Out</u> (Notarius, Ph.D., and Markman, Ph.D., 1993) address the various styles of conflict; we learn to put ourselves in the other person's shoes, tune into our inner voice, identify the thoughts that arouse us, and transform anger into words. In <u>I Thought We'd Never Speak Again</u> (2003), Laura Davis talks about discerning the real problem and our role in it, the value of persistence and forgiving others, and the need to establish autonomy and set appropriate boundaries. Finally, in <u>Beyond Blame</u> (1994), Kottler suggests past relationships influence how we deal with present conflict situations. Kottler advocates identifying what sets us off, understanding the origins and causes of our conflicts, taking responsibility instead of blaming others, and making the changes we need to stop repeating the past.

The third group is a hybrid of the other two, probably the best example being <u>Difficult Conversations</u> by Stone, Patton, and Heen (1999). Books in this category offer us tools *and* introspection, often highlighting the importance of "relationship." They provide techniques – such as asking open-ended questions, mapping each party's contribution to the current situation, seeing the problem from another point of view, distinguishing between the message intended and the message delivered – as well as emphasize the role of perceptions, the need to express and listen to feelings, the importance of understanding why what's being said bothers us, and how conflict clashes with our feelings of self-worth, competence, and inner goodness.

Tough Times Call for a Different Understanding

All of these books are right – they are useful, creative, and well worth reading. Yet, they haven't changed how we talk with one another and deal with differences. It was back in 1979 when Richard Bolton first wrote his book on people skills. Titled, <u>People Skills – How to Assert Yourself, Listen to Others and Settle Disputes</u>, it was chock-full of ideas for active listening, facilitating dialogue, and improving our overall communication skills. Yet, like so many of the more recent books, it wasn't enough. Poorly managed conflict seems more prevalent today than ever and invades every sphere of our lives – at work, at home, on the road, over health care, between religious and ethnic groups, with other countries, among blocs of nations; we conflict with our bodies, our most intimate partners, and our environment.

There could be several explanations for this. Perhaps, most lay-people don't read conflict management books and instead, these books are preaching to a choir of professional problem-solvers. Perhaps the tools are too difficult to put into practice, especially when the stakes are high and we need them most. Perhaps we are too quick to conflict. In any given situation, we *do* tend to perceive a disagreement as a win/lose proposition, so we start with something at risk. We assume there are two sides to every conflict and are quick to take up a position. We think in terms of one solution, one right answer to solve the problem. Perhaps, too, conflict is offering us a lesson we're simply not learning.

The lesson conflict has to teach us is crucial to what happens next to humanity. We are on the brink of some pretty tough times – times that promise to convince us of our interdependence. They will be characterized by globalization, climate change, and diversification; a new and changing balance of world power, wealth, and natural resources; and a plethora of deeply polarized views and many, many interconnected problems that need solving. These tough times will demand cooperation at every level. They will require a different kind of people skills: skills specifically aimed at *helping us get along*. For that reason, this book builds on all of these other texts and attempts to take one small, yet significant step forward: it suggests that conflict is an opportunity to increase **awareness**. It suggests that learning to deal with differences is more than knowing what we need, understanding the other person's reality, and resolving the problem-at-hand. It's a chance to move beyond "me", and "you", and even "us", and the underlying mind-set that is dominated by the ego. It's a chance to get outside ourselves; to be transpersonal, if you will.

That does not mean that conflict will lead straight to enlightenment; that you should quick, go don your robes and take a meditative stance. Not at all. This is a practical book that will show you how dealing with differences can help you be a better person; how you can learn something about yourself and your relationship with others while you decrease the number and intensity of negative conflict situations you encounter; and how to find a higher ground where you can talk with anyone.

A transpersonal world view is one that appreciates different truths. When applied to conflict, it's a change in thinking that's pragmatic and positive. A transpersonal discussion works towards civility while accepting that conflict isn't pretty; encourages people to solve their own problems, without relying on outside intervention; emphasizes the need to hear first and be heard, without needing to know the answer; assumes an abundance of solutions and a longer horizon for decision-making; and views every set of differences as the potential for a shift in awareness, *beyond ourselves*. People skills are the skills we need to get along in the world. They are parenting skills, motivational skills, and peace-making skills. They are the heart of intimate partnerships, business relationships, and international alliances...and absent them, the cause of failed marriages, broken contracts, and cold wars. This book asks a very basic question: what can we do – besides argue – when people disagree with us? The answer can literally change your life.

Reading This Book

This book is heavily influenced by the work of Baruch A. Bush and Joseph P. Folger in Transformative Mediation. It also weaves in thinking from the Eastern traditions, the healing sciences, and Transpersonal Psychology, which are increasingly being looked to by mediators and others as important sources of ideas, insights, and inspiration. It is the result of listening to hundreds of hours of family mediation and many years of trying to manage public sector squabbles. The intended audience is lay problem-solvers; professionals in their own right, who, as part of their job, have to resolve conflict...people such as parents, bosses, supervisors, religious leaders, school board members, elected officials, town clerks, teachers, CEO's, and group leaders. While this book offers tools, they are embedded in a broader understanding which makes the tools easier to recall and apply. For that reason, the book has wide application for professionally trained problem-solvers as well; in particular, those who are just starting out and those who have been at it for a long time.

The book covers three broad areas: the first and second sections focus on the individual, the third addresses our relationships, and the final section deals with conflict on the world stage. Chapter One covers some basic, concrete tools for managing conflict. It is largely tactical and while it won't change the world, it will help you, the reader, begin to approach conflict differently. Some of the tools are self-evident, and yet, rarely applied. By the end of the first chapter, you will find yourself thinking about conflict in a new light, and ready for Chapter Two. Chapter Two explains why even the best outfitted tool box isn't enough. It argues that we need a different framework through which to view conflict and the world, and through such a framework, we can more naturally apply our tools.

That framework is presented and developed in Chapter Three which examines the sources of conflict and why we act the way we do. Chapter Three introduces the idea of *self proving*. Self proving is what we usually do in the face of differences; how we fall back on well-worn patterns that have rarely worked in the past in the hopes that things will turn out differently this time. There are many ways to address self proving. Most importantly, we need to shift how we interact with the world around us – we need to grow more aware. Chapter Four describes the first techniques for doing so and presents several ideas for how to begin to chip away at ego-dominated conflict. It also provides the first of three keys to getting along in tough times.

Chapters Five and Six explore different kinds of relationships: one-on-one relationships and those between intimate partners, parents, co-parents, and families. Particular emphasis is placed on the role of emotions and doing just the opposite of what we normally do in an argument: drawing emotions out. These chapters also consider the natural process of contraction, and cover the second key to getting along. Chapter Seven places our relationships in a larger context, setting the stage for Chapter Eight which examines our relationships at work and group dynamics – from yoga class to the corner office.

Chapters Nine and Ten consider conflict in the world and the institutional form of self-proving. In these chapters we examine how the framework applies to world affairs and what each of us can do to make a difference. These chapters offer the third and final key to getting along. Intermingled throughout the book are new and different techniques, tools, and ideas for dealing with conflict, important questions to ask, and ways to reaffirm our commitment to a shift in awareness.

The goal of this book is to foster a different way of talking with one another, and in particular, for dealing with differ-ences. The measures of success are quite simple:

- Were the people involved able to solve their problem, their way?
- Was the relationship maintained or improved as a result? And,
- Did we collectively gain in awareness to help us face the future?

If so, you know the keys to getting along. You have the people skills you'll need for tough times.

Section One

Changing Your Life

Chapter 1

The Basic Tools for Getting Along

Three professional couples are sitting in a restaurant. One woman is discussing her new assignment and the myriad tasks she needs to complete in a very compressed time frame. Suddenly, she turns to the woman sitting beside her and says:

"And I have something *you* can do as well."

What did she mean by that? Did she mean she had something particularly difficult for this other woman to do? Something that required her very unique skills set and wealth of expertise? Did she mean she had something that *even* this woman could do? Was she saying the other woman wasn't working hard enough or should be busier? Or the work she was doing wasn't worth her while? Was she suggesting the other woman should be working *for her?* Would she pay her...enough?

Why Conversation Matters

How we talk to one another says something important about us. It's a reflection of who we are and a predictor of our quality of life. It says something about person-kind as well: it's a measure of how far we've evolved as human beings and whether we're living up to our full potential.

As even this simple exchange suggests, conversation often involves a fair amount of confusion, and with enough confusion, comes conflict. The problem begins with the assumption that the point of having a conversation is to tell someone something. In fact, that's only half the point: the other person has something to tell us as well. It may be something we want to hear or something we're afraid to face; something to do with what we're talking about or an issue totally unrelated. In the frantic pace of living our lives, one-half of nearly every conversation gets lost. We start with this wrong notion about why we're having a conversation and the situation deteriorates from there.

It's probably a hard-sell to suggest that conflict is an opportunity in disguise. When someone says something hurtful, questions our judgment, walks out in anger, or challenges something we hold dear, it's hard to see conflict as a chance. But it is. It's a chance to learn about ourselves, try something different, test our assumptions, and ultimately, move beyond our current level of awareness. How many times have we asked, "Yes, but how can I make a difference? How can one person have an impact?" Changing the way we deal with differences is one answer to that question. It's about so much more than resolving the issue-at-hand; it's a chance to change our lives, our minds, and the world.

So It Goes

Despite the importance of conversation, we don't spend a lot of time thinking about how we talk to one another. Rather, much of what we say and do is based on *habit*. In a typical conversation, we are driven by our habits and assumptions, and by what we think we know about other people. Most of the time, we're on automatic pilot.

Generally speaking, we enter into a conversation assuming what we have to say is important and expecting the other person to understand and agree with us. Perhaps we want to tell a story or talk about an upcoming presentation. We may need a report done in a particular way or want to review specific information as soon as possible. We may want to talk about how we feel, how hurt we were by what happened, or our need for more respect, appreciation, or time together. There may be a cause we feel passionate about, a critical matter that needs clearing up, or an irritating problem with a supervisor or a teenager that needs to be addressed right away.

When people don't agree with us, we feel uncomfortable. Their lack of validation introduces a certain tension into the conversation. If the conversation is an important one and/or the person we're speaking to is someone we value, we instinctively try to "right" the situation. We may say something to protect our feelings or justify our position. We may restate our point of view, believing the other person disagrees with us because she doesn't understand. We may speak louder or move-in closer, hoping she will hear us more clearly and then concede the point. Under the right conditions, our attempts fail and the tension escalates. We find ourselves needing to prove what we're saying is right and important. Unfortunately, she feels the exact same way, fearing her point is equally lost on us. The net result is conflict.

Consider the following situation:

You're having a conversation with a colleague at work about the provisions of an important contract. He says something that strikes you as odd: that he doesn't want "to repeat the same mistakes the company made in the last contract. That was disastrous." The comment stays with you and later you think, "Hey, I supervised that contract and it was perfectly fine." So you set it aside. The next time you see this person, you approach him with a slightly different frame of mind; you expect that he may say something offensive. If he does or you perceive that he does, you put the two events together. You might try to confront him with his poor opinion of you or his offensive style, but he doesn't seem to be listening or he sloughs it off, saying you're too sensitive or defensive.

In time, you begin to dread seeing this guy. You avoid working with him on projects; talk to others about how unreasonable and irritable he is, and suspect everything he says as malicious. One day, he undermines your authority right in front of a staff person and you erupt...not just over the event but over the whole history that's accumulated between the two of you. You rally your co-workers around you and proceed to list the numerous infractions he's committed. He is profoundly dumbfounded; as are you, at his surprise. You decide there's no working with this guy and write him off as that "a—— at work."

Sound familiar? Everyone has at least one such experience. It might be with an uncle or a sibling, an ex-spouse, a parent, a boss, a former best friend, a neighbor, or the budget chairperson at church. We didn't want it to turn out that way but, so it goes.

Positional Bargaining

Most of us only know one way to deal with differences. It's called *positional bargaining*. In positional bargaining, we quickly frame an opinion, stake out a position, and consider that to be our best and final thinking on the matter. There are two "sides" in a positional argument and each holds an immutable position that is diametrically opposed to the other. From both inside and outside the argument, there appears to be no common ground and no room for compromise. Rather than work together, "Each negotiator asserts what he will and won't do...and tries through sheer will power to force the other to change its position" (Ury and Fisher, 1981, pp. 6). The two sides' trade attacks and counter-attacks, expert witnesses and contrary opinions, proposed concessions and counter-proposals – all the while remaining wholly committed to their position. To even consider a compromise would be to abandon one's principles (Moore, 2003, pp. 277). There's a lot at stake in positional bargaining.

Positional bargaining is all about power and control: winning means the other party must lose. The classic case is two parents fighting over the custody of a child where both parents want full custody; or, in a joint custody situation, each parent wants exactly 50 percent of the child's time – down to the minute. It's even worse in group setting or a conflict among countries, where participants are bolstered by a kind of "group-think" mentality and spur one another on, hurling insults and accusations across picket lines, public hearing rooms, and negotiating tables.

In many respects, positional bargaining is socially ingrained. It is certainly the basis of most sports activities: one team wins and the other loses. The legal system too, is frequently seen as a win-lose proposition: parties come to court ready to "fight to the finish", only to learn that few people have the resources to do so. Positional bargaining can also be the negotiating style of some attorneys: "Lawyers who have been trained to develop an argument that supports a singular outcome" may see issues and options in "yes-or-no terms", and assume a posture of "hard-line" positional bargaining (Moore, 2003, pp. 150).

Once articulated, positional bargainers become so vested in their positions, they leave little room for themselves to back off, making it nearly impossible to explore what's driving those positions and/or what else might be important. Often, it becomes necessary to bring in an outsider to force the parties to reach "a settlement". They may split the difference or, if the problem is value-laden, agree to disagree. Invariably, regardless of how the situation is settled, both sides claim victory and accuse the other of negotiating in bad faith.

Most of us resort to positional bargaining out of habit – it's what we do when people disagree with us. Yet its use is not restricted to individuals or small groups. Consider the following positional tactics of President Bush and the United States Congress, between March and May of 2007, with respect to the continued funding bill for the Iraq War. According to the headlines and text of <u>The NY Times</u>, the following debate ping-ponged across the national stage:

<u>March 12.</u> The President wants an Iraq funding bill with "no strings attached."

<u>March 24.</u> The Democrats feel they "rode to power last November on the public's discontent with the war in Iraq." They need to tie an "exit strategy" to funding in order to meet voter demands.

<u>March 27.</u> The Senate opens debate on the $122 billion Iraq spending bill; "Republicans to rely on 'President's veto' versus 'procedural maneuvers' to block Congress from imposing a withdrawal date for the troops."

<u>March 27.</u> On the same day, "In a Pew Research Center poll, 60% of Americans say they want Congress to support a troop withdrawal by August, 2008."

<u>March 28.</u> Senate supports a pull-out date.

<u>March 29.</u> President rules out bid by Congress for Iraq pull-out.

<u>March 31.</u> Headlines read, "Army's War Funds Can Last thru July."

<u>April 1.</u> Iraq bill is called a "vote to no-where."

<u>April 4.</u> Headlines warn "Political brinksmanship intensifies."

<u>April 11.</u> Bush "accused Democrats in Congress of behaving irresponsibly, invites leaders of both parties to 'discuss ways forward' but has no

intention of using session to negotiate or compromise."

<u>April 17.</u> Bush "leans on Democrats with talk of
troops suffering."

<u>April 20.</u> Senate Majority Leader Harry Reid states,
"This war is lost."

<u>April 25.</u> Bush/Cheney "aggressively challenge" the
motives of Congressional Democrats.

<u>April 27.</u> Senate passes bill; Bush has promised to
veto: "The White House called it a 'defeatist
strategy' that insists on a date for surrender,
micro-manages our commanders and gener-
als...and adds billions of dollars in unrelated
spending."

Senate Majority Leader Harry Reid states, "We
have carried forth the wishes of the American
people."

<u>April 28.</u> The headlines shift: Congress and the
President have "toned down the talk and hinted
at a willingness to compromise"... "The challenge now is to bridge the gap between hard
and fast positions."

<u>May 2.</u> Reuters reports, "Bush/Democrats begin to
search for Iraq compromise."

This is the flow of a typical positional argument. It's about
winning and losing, persuasion and tactics, and right and
wrong. It's often loud, contentious, combative, and hurtful.
When we deal with differences in this way, we are too quick
to conflict. We forfeit half of the conversation, lose sight of
the things we really want and need, and constrict our range
of options. Oftentimes, we end up feeling bad about ourselves
and isolated from others. To make matters worse, when we
argue positions, nobody really wins.

Some Life Changing Tools

When we think about changing how we talk with one another, we naturally gravitate to the idea of tools. The hope is that with a couple of solid tools, we can avoid positional bargaining and maybe conflict altogether. The tools that follow can be used alone, or, more aptly, as a precursor to the rest of the book, as a complement to people skills for tough times. What makes these tools unique is that they create a momentary distance between us and the conversation. That distance alone, can begin to change our life.

Tool #1. Choose Your Hills Carefully

It's amazing the number of things we can overlook. We can overlook the sexist comment an older friend makes who we know, just doesn't understand and probably never will. We can overlook the Ph.D. who repeatedly tells us how "college level" courses are organized; as though she's the only one who's ever attended. We can overlook an unconscious manager's refusal to get our name right or appreciate our work. We can especially overlook a dear friend, as at the beginning of this Chapter, who's so absorbed in her new assignment that she's too tired to think straight.

There are also many things we don't need to say. We don't need to comment on what another person is buying, or eating, or wearing, or feeling. We don't need to respond to everything that's said *to* us; or *about* us, or, that we think has been said about us or might be said about us at some point in the future. We don't need to fill up empty air-time, or talk because we're ill-at-ease, embarrassed, or confused.

In other words, a lot of what sticks to us doesn't have to. Because we're living at hyper-speed, in constant touch but not connected, we forget that many of the things we allow to upset us can just be let go. Tool #1 suggests we take a moment to first examine whether we can overlook what's been said or done, and simply, release it. We can reflect on the many reasons why it may have been said. We can consider when it was said; that perhaps, under different circumstances, it wouldn't bother us at all. As a general rule, if we don't suffer, let it go.

Tool #2. Tune Into The "Shift"

Every conversation has the potential to warp into an argument, and as such, harbors a moment when things begin to shift. It's the point at which we sense an inner un-ease, but before we actually take offense or feel a need to reply to what's been said or done. Tool #2 asks us to start to look for this shift in our conversations and take time to study it. This is the turning point in the conversation when we elect to enter into what could become a heated debate.

Choosing to engage in a conflict situation isn't a "bad" choice. It's simply a choice. If we choose to enter, it's best to view the conversation as an engagement between two people who are trying to understand something together. This is true even if the other person doesn't see it this way. On the other hand, we can be aware of the shift and choose *not* to enter. In that case, we need to be aware how easy it is to be drawn into an argument. If, for example, someone says, "I've been having some emotional issues lately," we can make a conscious decision not to enter this discussion. We might say, "I'm sorry you've been having some tough times," or, "Well, you're always pretty good at working those through," or, more honestly, "I'm wondering if there's another time to talk about this or another person you might talk with?"

Tool #3. How You Say It Matters

Tool #3 is all about using positive language. How we say what we need to say requires some foresight and some thought; we need to think about it in advance and entertain some options. For example,

- a health care clinic can be described as serving the community with an array of family planning, AIDS prevention, contraception, and S.T.D. prevention services, or, providing "abortion-on-demand";
- a political candidate can be portrayed as being a crime fighter, cleaning up skid row, and saving the city, or, as an insensitive marital partner, who did a flip-flop on abortion, and is wishy-washy on same sex marriage;
- a national Department of Peace can be characterized as a viable alternative and balanced complement to the Department of Defense, or, something that appeals to a "bunch of wusses."

Language is a key part of getting along. We need to be aware of how we say things, the language we're accustom to using, and the language we hear around us every day. In a difficult conversation, for example, we won't be successful trying to fully script in advance what we're going to say, or using language we're not familiar with. Nor is it advisable to use inflammatory language, emotionally-charged phrases, or terms and words we know will trigger or grate on the other party.

Tool #3 says: choose the timing, the setting, and words with care. As a rule of thumb, positive language inspires the conversation to continue; albeit in a heated, but non-destructive way. If, however, the other person walks out or immediately retaliates in-kind, language has failed everyone involved.

Tool #4. Be Transparent. Period.

This is perhaps, the most important tool on this list because it forces us to take a break, reach inside, and then articulate what we're experiencing. Being transparent means expressing what's going on for us in the conversation – how we're feeling, what we're experiencing, and what our reality is right now. Being transparent is not about how we think the other person is *making* us feel; it's about how we feel. For example,

– "I'm feeling pretty annoyed right now."
– "Whoa, I'm totally embarrassed."
– "You're right. I'm not prepared today."
– "I'm ashamed this happened."
– "I'm really nervous and scared.
– "That felt really hurtful to me. Is that what you meant?"

Being transparent is important because it slows the tempo of the conversation and candidly states a fact. Consider the following scenario:

Friend 1:"Do you have any idea how important this job is to me? I've been stuck in this house for three years. I need your support and all you've done is put me down. You're just jealous and angry that I'm moving on and you're not. What on earth do you want from me?"

Friend 2: "What the hell are you talking about? I'm not jealous or angry. I just think this job is beneath you. You've got all this talent and it's going to go to waste there. I don't want you stuck in the house but don't settle for something that's beneath you."

Is this second comment transparent? Will it inflame the discussion or encourage it to continue in a non-destructive way? What if, instead, Friend 2 tried:

Friend 2: "I'm not feeling jealous or angry. I'm feeling scared. I don't want you stuck in the house. I'm just afraid that when you go back to work, we won't see each other very much, and we'll grow apart. That's all."

This second effort is transparent, it's real. It defuses the tension in the conversation and encourages it to proceed. It invites Friend 1 to be transparent too; it says: *it's safe to be honest here.*

Tool #5. Make Sure You've Heard What Was Said

This is an old tool, sometimes called "active listening." It requires that when someone is finished speaking, we restate what's been said to ensure we've heard it correctly. Tool #5 avoids introducing confusion into a conversation because if something has been misunderstood, it can be cleared up immediately.

Tool #5 also bars us from hearing what we want to hear. This is especially true for couples when one person has moved on and the other is still attached. We need to remember, no matter how clearly something is stated, if someone wants to believe otherwise, he/she will. Consider the following:

Wife: "You're right. This has been extremely difficult and having to move the kids out of the house and be there for them 24/7 with no help at all,

has made my life nearly impossible. Sometimes I don't know if I can't live with *or* without you. This has been hard on everybody, especially the kids."
Husband: "So you *have* thought about us getting back together?"

The husband has an option here. Instead of tuning in to what's most important to him – whether there's a chance of them getting back together – he could have tried an active listening response, such as,
Husband: "I can't even imagine. You must be exhausted."

Most importantly, Tool #5 keeps our attention in the conversation. We have to pay attention in order to re-state what's been said. We can't be thinking about our counter-offer, how to spread the blame, or what we're going to say next. Active listening forces us to be right there.

Tool #6. Don't Be Surprised.

Conversations, especially difficult ones, shouldn't be full of surprises. We need to consider the other party and take some time to contemplate the situation from his/her point of view. In this respect, it's useful to recall three simple rules:

(1) Come with one or more proposals, anticipate how the other person will respond to them, and have ideas for how to address his/her concerns;

(2) Know in advance, where or how we are, or might be, considered responsible for the present situation. Be ready to respond to whatever accusations might arise without becoming defensive;

and, finally,

(3) Understand that reaching an agreement is not the same as the other person agreeing with what we want! It's a give and take, an exchange of ideas.

Tool #7. Set A Goal of Comfort.

Not every discussion will end well, not every argument can be avoided, and not every conflict can be resolved. Nevertheless, the goal should be to keep the relationship alive, so we can continue to work together, visit and see one another, and be in one another's company. In fact, it's a good idea to assume we will *have* to continue to work together or be in one another's company, and allow that awareness to shape how we deal with differences. Before we say or do something, think: how will this affect our future relationship?

In the same vein, it's important that every argument include an ending ritual, a way to formally close the discussion. We should have as our intent, that both parties participate in the ritual as a chance to "put it all behind us." Go out for a drink, have a party, burn a hateful note – something that allows both people to consciously acknowledge, "that's over, now let's move on."

Chapter 2

More than Tools

Unfortunately, tools are never enough.

Tools are easily forgotten, especially when the stakes are high and what's being said offends us. Tools can feel scripted or phony. They can force us to do something that's out of character, or trigger a surprise response we're not prepared for. Tools aren't enough for dealing with differences for the same reason they're not enough to protect the environment or save a marriage: without being grounded in something that gives them meaning, tools are just mechanical. And conflict is much more than mechanics.

The fact is most of us already know the core instructions for resolving conflict without resorting to positional bargaining. We know we should spend most of our time defining the problem, brainstorm plausible solutions without judgment, choose the best solutions, and test our results. Recently, even more elaborate alternative conflict resolution models have become commonplace. The U.S. Navy, for example, has such a program, the basic principles of which include:

(1) Think Before Acting...Consider the Opportunities, Weigh the Possibilities;

(2) Listen Actively;

(3) Assure a Fair Process;

(4) Attack the Problem, Not Each Other;

(5) Accept Responsibility rather than Assess Blame;

(6) Use Direct Language;

(7) Emphasize Interests rather than Positions;

(8) Focus on the Future, What You Can Do Differently Tomorrow; and,

(9) Consider Solutions that Foster Mutual Gain (See USNavy.org).

So why don't we follow these instructions? They seem simple enough. Why isn't it second nature to think, "Hey, I've got to work with this guy, I better handle this situation with that in mind"? Why are we instead, so quick to take up sides and forge a position? The answer is in part due to the nature of conflict.

It's a Tough World Out There

The nature of conflict is to *escalate*. From start to finish, conflict naturally picks up speed and gains momentum: it becomes more intense, more personal, and more boisterous; it grows more aggressive, offensive, and harsh. Before you can catch it, it's out of control. Think for a moment, about just the *sound* of conflict:

Muffled noises, slightly raised voices, then periods of silence. Someone sounds hurt; he seems to be dominating the conversation. He's talking louder now. The other person "shushes." Then she throws a zinger: her tone changes, body shifts, intonation becomes more severe. The pitch becomes strident: they talk faster, talk over one another, and talk *loud*. Someone raises an issue from the past – her mother, his inability to discipline the kids...her bad choices, his instability...her sloppy house, his affair – the words seem to resonate in the room. They hurl accusations, threaten to leave, slam doors, scream in frustration, and leave in a huff.

Or, perhaps, the anger is the quiet kind:

There's silence; heavy, tense silence. Anger hangs in the air, ready to erupt at any moment. It's full of pain and resentment. The tension bubbles just beneath the surface, is thinly papered over when friends arrive, and then returns with a vengeance. It mounts with time, laden with fear, thick with anticipation. There's so much to say, but no-one-says-a-word. They wait for someone to rip open the wound.

Conflict naturally escalates: people have conversations, someone gets offended, he/she gets defensive, voices are raised, and an argument ensues; a group launches a project, opinions clash over how to do it, opposing forces align, factions undermine one another, and a dispute ensues; countries have different agendas, they trade accusations, publicly taunt and deride one another, make obligatory attempts at diplomacy, and an altercation ensues. Even the words we use reflect this penchant; they're action words, often laced with violence.

We:
- Demand our rights
- Dominate the discussion
- Defend our principles
- Intimidate the opposition
- Assert pressure
- Exact a confession
- Exert control
- Retaliate in-kind

We:
- Attack the problem
- Prosecute the offender
- Attempt a hostile takeover
- Challenge policies
- Engage in predatory practices

33

- Settle scores
- Cross-examine the witness
- Wage wars

Conflict escalation is part of our social mind set. Three conditions make this so. First, we pride ourselves on our individuality – we value our opinions and take it personally when others don't. We also prize our creativity and problem-solving skills. Second, we instinctively compare ourselves to others – our values, resources, and successes. We strive to work the hardest, stay the youngest, and be the smartest. Finally, competition is endemic to how we live. It's the engine of our economic and political systems. We compete for jobs, trophies, and stuff...to spread democracy, the word of God, and our way of life. Taken together – our pride in individuality, tendency to compare, and competitive nature – once it starts, conflict naturally escalates.

Yet this escalation also *separates* us. It divides us into Us and Them, all or nothing, with or against, right and wrong. It creates winners and losers; haves and have-nots. It labels some people criminals and others, judges; some immigrants and others, aliens; some heroes, others terrorists. One could argue we are living in a chronic state of separateness: separated from nature, from the results of our actions, and from one another.

Interests-Based Negotiations

When an argument picks up speed in an already racing world, it's a hard thing to stop. Its little wonder our tools fail: against such an onslaught, tools that aren't grounded in substance and meaning don't stand a chance. Yet, positional bargaining is not our only option. Many scholars and practitioners alike have designed alternative ways to deal with conflict and its natural escalation. Each reflects a different perspective on the causes of conflict, a unique world view, and some thoughts on human nature.

Positional bargaining is often contrasted with what's known as *interests-based negotiations*. In an interests-based approach, it's not positions that are at stake in a conflict situation, but "interests". Interests are the wants and needs that lie beneath and drive our positions. Ideally, in interests-based negotiations, each party seeks to uncover and express its interests such that an agreement can be crafted that meets everyone's needs. Concessions can be traded, accommodations can be made, and parties can "get to yes" without having to escalate to positional bargaining.

"Interests" are a lot trickier than positions. Positions are generally known in advance and rehearsed mentally, with co-workers and friends. Positions sound rational and right, even catchy; people can rally behind a position. Interests, on the other hand, are generally unknown. They need to be discovered, and sometimes, admitted to. In the classic case of two parents fighting over the custody of a child, the issue may be less about having full custody than about wanting *what full custody says* about them: that they're good parents, loving people, and wonderful with the children...that they couldn't possibly be at fault for the divorce.

Whereas positional bargaining sees the world in terms of finite resources which must be carefully divided, interests-based negotiations expand the range of available solutions. For example, to frame a problem as "to close or not close the school" restricts options, whereas seeing it as a matter of decreasing budget expenditures, coordinating resources, or other related interests, multiplies the possibilities. Similarly, couples can go numerous rounds in a divorce battle arguing over who gets the house, without realizing what they really want is for the other person to admit they had some good times together. Once expressed, the house issue is easily resolved.

Interests are the needs that must be met for people to be at peace with whatever the problem is, and let it go. Since most people are not aware of their interests, it's often necessary to have an outside person, such as a mediator, assist parties in defining and clarifying their interests; and then help meld those interests into viable solutions. Whether an outside mediator is involved or not, most of the material written today about mediation and conflict resolution emphasizes the importance of identifying interests. Doing so avoids having to split the difference and goes instead, for a "win-win."

Other Ways to Deal with Differences

Two other approaches for dealing with conflict will be mentioned here. While both are styles of mediation, each offers tools and ideas easily adapted for personal use.

The less well-known of the two is called *strategic* conflict resolution. The strategic style views conflict as caused by an underlying or latent problem which is unknown to the parties. Since the problem keeps interfering with the discussion, it must be surfaced and addressed before constructive problem-solving can ensue (Kressel, 2007, pp. 252, 273). In strategic negotiations, emphasis is placed on "diagnosing" the hidden problem which requires the help of an outside mediator who is specially trained to be highly directive. Through a process of "persistent and structured question asking" (ibid., pp. 267), the mediator helps the parties identify the problem and then strategize how to resolve it.

Obviously, deciphering interests (as in interests-based negotiations) or diagnosing underlying causes (as in strategic negotiations) is much more difficult than blindly adhering to a position. However, interests-based and strategic negotiations share a common drawback: they risk overlooking the emotional dimension of conflict. In contrast, the *transformative* style pays particular attention to emotions and the importance of preserving the relationship. Pioneered by Baruch Bush and Joseph Folger, Transformative Mediation (TM) is based on the relational view of human nature. According to this view, the core of human nature is comprised of a "dual sense" of individuality and social connectedness (Bush and Folger, 2005, pp. 59-61, [citing Della Noce, 1999]). Since conflict negatively affects both aspects, we find it unsettling and disturbing. In other words, conflict makes us feel bad. Bush and Folger argue that conflict is more than a matter of interests or latent, hidden problems: it's the impact conflict has on us as individuals and on our relationships that matters most. They suggest that what bothers people most about conflict is:

> That it leads and even forces them to behave towards themselves and others in ways that they find uncomfortable and even repellent... [they feel alienated from] their own strength and...sense of connection to others" (ibid., pp. 45-6).

Under the transformative model, conflict is seen as a "crisis in relationship", where "learning to live with no" can be just as important as "getting to yes". Early-on in the conflict cycle, people feel weak and self-absorbed and are unwilling to hear anything but their own story. Ideally, by enabling parties to make their own decisions and listen – when and if they're ready – the people involved can begin to feel stronger as individuals and more responsive to one another (ibid., pp. 55). They can transform the nature of their "conflict interaction" from a negative to a more positive and constructive experience.

One factor particularly distinctive about the transformative model is how it deals with emotions. Conventional wisdom tells us that in an argument, anger should be diffused, differences should be minimized, and emotions should be kept in check. Most of us try to avoid overt displays of emotions in our personal and professional life. An emotional outburst at work, for example, is generally regarded as unacceptable, and how often have we heard – or said – "we'll finish this when you're not so emotional"?

This is true of most styles of mediation as well. Interests-based mediators, for example, are instructed in specific strategies for suppressing negative emotions and de-escalating emotional outbursts. As author Christopher Moore explains: "Expression of strong negative emotions...has value only if it permits a productive physiological release" and only so long as it doesn't harm the already "delicate" relationship between the parties (Moore, 2003, pp. 174); which is to say, so long as it doesn't jeopardize reaching a resolution. Similarly, mediators who use the strategic style focus on:

> [Helping] parties solve an immediate practical concern... [whereas] hidden, problematic aspects of the party's circumstances or relationship that are not relevant...are ignored (Kressel, 2007, pp. 255).

Under the transformative approach, mediators are taught to "lean into" emotions whenever emotions are present. This does not mean mediators ask probing questions or try to diagnose latent problems. Better said, Transformative Mediators don't shy away from emotions. If emotions are expressed, a party might be asked if he/she wants to say *more* about what they're feeling. In a TM session, people are free to express their emotions, talk about the past, and/or "rail at the world" until they're finished doing so. The hope is that they can then let go of such feelings because the emotional charge has been released. In TM, the goal of preserving the relationship takes precedence over coming up with a solution. Or, to put it another way, the relationship is more important than the problem.

A Fresh Look

Obviously, many people have thought long and hard about conflict and various ways to resolve it. By now, one thing should be apparent: *differences are normal.* Differences happen; they *should* happen. They are part of living as a group. They shouldn't surprise us or be avoided. Unfortunately, "I hate confrontation. I avoid it at all costs" is an all too common refrain. But by avoiding conflict, we actually contribute to its escalation because we're not dealing with it; we're not doing what needs to be done. Nor should differences be a source of shame. Differences add diversity; they give breadth and depth to living.

On one level, dealing with differences is a matter of power and control. It's about the persuasiveness of our argument and the power of our presentation; the interests that drive us, the problems that get in our way, and the relationships we value. Yet, it's also about perceptions and feelings that get stuck, assumptions that are locked in place, and behavior that needs to change. For the tools in Chapter One to be of real value, we need a different way of looking at conflict, its causes, and its resolution. In particular, we need an understanding of conflict that:

(1) Builds on what's come before, on what interests-based, Transformative Mediation, and other approaches have taught us;

(2) Begins with individuals – our beliefs, perceptions, and feelings – such that through our individual actions, we can affect how conflict is dealt with in relationships, groups, and across cultures; and,

(3) Fully appreciates the escalatory nature of conflict and the way we live, how conflict divides and separates us, and the lesson it has to teach us.

The remainder of this book seeks to build such an understanding. It suggests one way of looking at conflict – not the right way or an altogether new way, but one way of thinking about conflict and its resolution. The book offers three keys to getting along. It also presents different "takes" on old ideas and numerous practical tools. Throughout the book are selected critical points which are designated in **bold** and *italics*, such as the fact that differences are normal. In addition, each chapter closes with a brief discussion of a topic area that considers conflict and the world from a very different perspective. One premise of this book is that change begets change – we need to challenge ourselves and our thinking in order to stay fresh and avoid growing rigid. These topical discussions represent areas for further exploration which the reader can pursue or not, depending on your choice.

Perhaps the best place to start is to reflect on how we, as individuals, contribute to the social mind set of conflict escalation....by not allowing ourselves enough time to get where we're going, accumulating more than we need, not giving someone a break in traffic, wearing clothes that are too tight, interrupting other people when they're talking, attending to our every "comfort need", replaying a story over and over in our heads, needing to buy "up" or buy more, driving aggressively, having yet another cup of coffee, needing to be first in line, talking too much/too often/too loud...how do you add to it?

AN AREA FOR FURTHER EXPLORATION

Kali-Yuga, Tough Times Indeed

Time can be calculated in many ways. According to ancient Indian Puranas (ancient classical works), "cosmic time is measured in terms of *yugas*... [which] are of four types, each of a different duration" (Muni, 2001, pp. 13). Within each yuga, there is expected to be "a corresponding physical and moral deterioration of the people living" during that time (ibid.). We are now said to be part of the second yuga type, characterized by the "rapid development of scientific knowledge, leading gradually into the occult" (Frawley, 1990, pp. 53).

Concurrently, we are part of the "longer age of Kali Yuga", wherein the "mentality of the majority of human beings...tends towards materialism" (ibid.). The "kali yuga is the Dark Age...destined to terminate in a convulsive cataclysm, accompanied by a major purging of humanity" (Feuerstein, 1996, pp. 9). It is for that reason that Hatha Yoga was created, "to serve the spiritual needs of people living in...[this] Dark Age of spiritual decline" (Feuerstein and Bodian, 1993, pp. 16). During this cosmic era, "we shall remain bound by time, undergoing continuous cycles of birth and death, until, in one lifetime we obtain liberation through the practice of yoga" (Muni, 2001, pp. 18).

Changing Your Mind

Chapter 3

The Source of Conflict

So far, we've learned we are too quick to conflict; that we often pick a side and argue a position. We've learned some tools that help by creating a momentary distance between us and an argument. We now know that conflict naturally escalates, and that this cycle of escalation isolates and separates us. This chapter looks at why all this is so, while Chapter Four begins to expand our resources for dealing with it.

When Good Goes Bad

A typical couple comes to mediation. They walk in – in silence – sit down and the argument begins:

Wife: "I cannot believe we're here, discussing this in front of a total stranger...this is so embarrassing. But you insisted, so I'm willing to give it a try; even though I think it's stupid. Anyway, the issue is I want him to put me on the deed to the house. We've been married for 5 years and I've paid towards the house, and I deserve to be on the–"

Husband: "I have told you a thousand times, get the title clear through an attorney and then we'll talk. But you never follow up, you never finish anything. You start things and you leave them. You–"

Wife: "Why should *I* get *your* title clear? And I did follow up and you have to sit down with your ex-wife and get her off the title."

Husband: "See, this is what I mean, communication. We simply do not communicate. That's why we're here. You need to learn to communicate. That's why this situation is such a mess, because you don't know how to talk."

Wife: "I know, I know. Blah, blah, blah. I have heard this refrain so often I could repeat it myself. And I talk fine, thank you very much. You're the one who doesn't talk. Look at your kids. Both of them are so screwed up – the school calls, their grades stink. What do you do? Not a thing. Do you sit down and talk with them? No. Do you help them with their school work? No. Do you explain why school is important? No. You need parenting classes or something. I should have seen this coming..."

Husband: "You're a fool. This marriage was fine until your daughter moved back into the house. You said before we were married, there was no chance of her moving back. Now we have that added expense. All I needed was another mouth to–"

Wife: "Another mouth? Are you insane? You follow her like the Gestapo. Turning down the heat, checking the frig, policing the thermostat day and night! You're nuts!"

Husband: "I'm nuts? What about all the time you spend with your friend Jennifer? Just what are you two doing toge–"

Wife: "You *are* crazy. You gamble our money away, and have the audacity to say something about me and a girlfriend? Like this situation is *my* fault? Who's to blame here, kiddo? I'm the one holding this marriage together; for what reason,

I don't know. And what right do you have to complain about what I do? You and your stupid motor-head friends. Nothing but a bunch of low-life jerks. At least with Jennifer, I'm working out at the gym and doing something construct–"

Husband: "*Our* money? Hold it. Hold everything! Did I hear you say, *our* money? You worked when we were first married. Now you sit around on your fat a–"

Wife: "Exactly. That's what this is about, isn't it? You thought you married a cash cow. You thought you'd have a constant source of income when you married me. Sometimes I wonder if that's the *only* reason you married me. You have been mean and insensitive since I went part-time. Well, *I* have records. *I* have documentation. I can prove how much I've put into this house. I financed all the landscaping, and re-did the living room. Without me, this house was a piece of –"

Husband: "That house is worth $180,000. Do you hear me? *I'm* worth something. I don't need your money. I am worth something. *You are not.* All you have is some measly bank account. I have a house. I have land."

Wife: "That's it, I knew it. This is all about money. You can't share your house because you can't share the money. You can't say, this is a partner–"

Husband: "You're an idiot. You need to learn to communicate. You need to get some psychiatric help. And you talk about my gambling, what about drinking in front of my boys? If anyone needs some parenting skills, it's you! You barely talk to your kids. I should have known this would be too much for you. You can't talk at home, there's

no reason to think you'd be able to here. I am
outta here. I have had it with you. Your records
are crap. I'm worth something. I have a home.
You're worth nothing." And he storms out.

A good argument lingers in the soul. It affects us mentally,
physically, and emotionally. What is it that could make two
people, once so excited about finding each other, so...rabid?

Self Proving

The answer is: self proving. Self proving is what we do whenever we feel threatened: someone says 'x', we feel threatened,
and we start inserting and asserting ourselves all over the place.
Human beings self prove all the time; its how we validate ourselves. But self proving is at its peak in conflict situations.

When we self prove, we're not reacting to a physical threat
but rather, an emotional one. We feel intimidated or afraid,
as though something's on the line and it is: our identity. Our
identity is how we see ourselves, our self image. Whenever our
identity feels threatened, challenged, or in any way, at risk, we
self prove:

- We assign blame, get defensive, and get angry;
- We jump to conclusions and make accusations;
- We generalize, stereotype, and judge others;
- We criticize, complain, and gossip to a friend;
- We insult, offend, and cut people down;
- We retaliate, stir the pot, or become abusive.

All of these are forms of self proving. They are also ways we
resist. Whenever we self prove, we are wholly self-absorbed and
trying to buck the flow.

This is the basic premise of the book: ***all conflict involves a
threat to our identity and we react to that threat by self proving***. While
our styles of self proving may differ considerably, there are cer-

tain characteristics common to all forms of self proving:

    (1) Self proving feels automatic: it happens before we're aware of it. Conscious thought seems to occur after the fact;

    (2) We are usually blind to the many ways we, personally, self prove. Often, we unknowingly project our flaws onto others;

    (3) Self proving sounds self righteous. We say and do whatever we can to justify or rationalize our position and behavior; and finally,

    (4) All self proving reflects a desire for control. There is an underlying assumption that we can, or need to, make the world a certain way.

A Self to Defend

Self proving begins with a self to defend. From the sum of our cultural and social conditioning, our life experiences, and our personal and universal proclivities, we each create a "self." The self is our organizing principle around which life evolves and revolves. It's the story of who we think we are: it's our identity.

Our self is different from everyone else. It's a person with a past and a future, a set of hopes and dreams, and a full complement of reasons, rationales, beliefs, opinions, judgments, and behavior. It's the result of our continuous experimentation in the world; the safety or danger we find there and internalize; the space we're given to try new things and fail; and the feedback we receive from others about who they want us to be, and what's appropriate, expected, and acceptable. Psychology suggests we spend the better part of the first quarter of life creating, casting, re-casting, and refining our sense of self. It's likely we spend the rest of our life validating it.

In large measure, we create a self through contrasts because duality is how the mind works: "The mind is a process, always changing... [there is] someone perceiving and something being perceived, someone thinking and something being thought" (Easwaran, 1992, pp. 153). Among the first contrasts we learn is to distinguish between "me" and "not-me":

> The newborn baby has little or no sense of identity... distinct from his surroundings...The infant adopts the distinctions of those who are taking care of him, and he makes other distinctions...as a result of his contact with the physical environment (Ajaya, 1983, pp. 127).

This fundamental distinction between "me" and "not me" stays with us throughout our lives, with "me" ending at my skin and "other" taking over from there; it's the first manifestation of our feeling of separateness, of disconnection. Over time, we come to see the world in contrasts as well: cause and effect, life and death, pleasure and pain, east and west, right and wrong, hot and cold, rational and emotional, heavy and light...like me or not like me, friend or enemy, war or peace.

As we grow, our self accumulates a history and a series of personal stories. We might see ourselves as a tower of strength, a pleaser or a giver, smart or elitist, or vindictive and cruel. We might believe we're a natural leader, a perfectionist, a procrastinator, an over-achiever, stoic, or carefree. Our stories are more detailed descriptions of who we think we are; an unabridged version of self. Taken together, the self contains everything we know about ourselves, and a great deal we don't. It embodies our childhood dramas, strengths and weaknesses, personal values, bedrock principles, and our deepest fears. It also includes our shadow opposite – the parts we have to work to uncover and know.

The self gives us an answer to life's first big question, "who am I?" As psychologist John Welwood tells us, we "try to defend and affirm [ourselves] by creating some stable self-existence"

(Welwood, 2000, pp. 26). Much of this identity revolves around two central questions, or *primary fears*. The first is the fear of non-existence. This fear continuously asks, "I'm here, right?" In later life, it becomes the seed of existential concerns about life's purpose and meaning. The second fear is the fear of isolation. The fear of isolation keeps asking, "I'm okay, right?" Throughout life, this fear conveys a need to belong and be accepted; to be part of a larger whole. These fears, and how we grapple with them, shape our development and mold our individual and social nature. Both are at the core of self proving.

Becoming Somebody

At first, the self feels like a fluid concept; we "try on" some characteristics and discard others. But in practically no time, we become *somebody*. Concepts ripen into values, goals become needs, and preferences develop into a personal sense of style. Where we once had desires, we now have expectations; what were once opinions are now judgments; and what used to be suggestions are now answers. The self becomes our identity – the image we must uphold – with an ego to help us do so. In time, the idea of "me" hardens down and our personal stories solidify. We become "*I*-centered", ego-centric: we begin to believe the world revolves around "me".

Our self is closely allied with the mind. It is dominated by thoughts and thinking; identified with the mind. There's a voice inside our heads that commentates our experience of living, telling us what's true and false, fair and unjust, right and wrong. The voice repeats and affirms our stories; our reasons, rationales, beliefs, opinions, judgments, and behaviors. It tells us what to expect and reassures us; that death is off sometime in the future, the other guy will be the one who gets sick, and we'll wake up in the morning...that some people will love us no matter what, we're in control of our destiny, and what we're experiencing is really happening.

Our thinking self also embraces a full set of assumptions about what we're entitled to and how things should be. Assumptions are unconscious rules we project onto the world but can't enforce. We assume we deserve happiness. We assume we're decent, intelligent, and rational people, who should be treated with respect, given a fair break, forgiven when we're wrong, and have an equal chance to succeed. We make assumptions about other people as well. Stereotypes, for example, are a type of assumption. We assume people are a certain way based on how they look, where and how they live, and what they do and say. All of this contributes to our sense of separation and isolation. According to Eckhart Tolle, as egos, we feel as "separate fragments...surrounded by other egos...with whom we have no connection" (Tolle, 1999, pp. 150).

Most importantly, we assume we're right. As ego-centered beings, we create a self to help give meaning to existence; to feel solid and secure, and give us something to hold on to; *and* to be right.

The Mind Contracts

The self is a gradual shrinking process: we shrink the entire range of possibilities down into this "self", and the full potential of who we could be down into "me". We then shrink the breadth of what's happening down into our understanding and experience of it. We filter some things out and highlight others. Eventually, we grow to rely on certain thoughts, desires, and behaviors more than others which, in time, form mental pathways in the mind. With continued use, these mental pathways become "conditioned, automatic ways of thinking and responding" (Easwaran, 1992, pp. 87). They become *mind ruts*: habits we return to again and again regardless of whether or not they work; restricted ways of thinking and behaving.

Whenever a series of mind ruts follow a similar stream, they converge to form the dominant patterns that seem to run our lives. Left unexamined, these patterns start to control our thoughts and dictate our behavior; the more ingrained they are, the easier they are to fall back into. Most of the time, we allow our mind ruts to take over and live in a kind of quasi-conscious, suspended state: on automatic pilot. Our personal opinions, likes and dislikes, beliefs, judgments, desires, attachments, behaviors – all of them mind ruts – seem to just happen. We think and reason, organize and reflect, compare and contrast, attach and repel, and remember it all, without too much conscious thought on our part. We *re-act* to life.

The First Mental Lock

When we hand our experience of living over to the mind and re-act to life, we start to believe we *are* the self and that this self is *real*. Many of us assume there's a little man at the controls, a conscience, a pilot making our decisions, perceiving the world, and generating ideas. But the self isn't real. Self, identity, ego, mind – they're just labels. They're concepts to help us understand. Yet, once we buy into the illusion that the self is real, we cut a devil's deal:

> The very power and control...acquired by drawing a boundary around oneself...[creates] its complement: an overwhelming sense of helplessness and weakness (Ajaya, 1983, pp. 128).

We grow more separate and alone. Moreover, we must maintain the illusion which requires our constant attention. We must continuously prop up and fortify the self, feeding it what it needs most: proof that we're okay...that we're here... that we're right...*self* proof.

As soon as we believe the self is real, the mind starts to lock in place. We engage a series of Mental Locks. A Mental Lock is an unconscious belief that helps prop up the self and our identity, which makes it incredibly powerful. Mental Locks keep us stuck in one place and lock out what really matters. Throughout the course of this book, we'll examine three Mental Locks especially relevant to conflict situations. The first is **we assume everyone sees the world as we do, or at least they should.** That's not to say we believe everyone agrees with us. Rather, we unconsciously believe that what we see as real is what everyone sees as real; that we all share the same experience of reality.

This is, perhaps, the ultimate state of self-absorption. This belief allows us to feel comfortable interpreting events and other people's behavior in ways that make sense to us. It perpetuates the belief that the world is solid, resources are scarce, and power and control are at a premium. It allows us to believe that with the right argument, people will understand our point of view, and ultimately, agree with us. And if they don't, it lets us write them off as stupid or not worth the trouble. By believing that everyone sees the world as we do, we can see the problem as being outside of ourselves and the skills to resolve it as inside. We can believe there is one truth.

Threatened and Re-Active

Conflict threatens our sense of self. It threatens the fundamental assumption that we share the same reality; that what we think and see is real. It triggers our primary fears and leaves us wondering…What if I'm not okay? What if I'm not here? Conflict undermines how we see ourselves and who we see ourselves to be. Even if the argument appears benign, it can feel like our very identity is at stake. If a problem is with a neighbor over a property line, it can feel like our integrity is at issue. In a staff meeting, it can feel like our judgment is being questioned. In a business deal, it can feel like our reputation is in jeopardy. In a group, while the discussion may be cold and factual, it can quickly devolve into a matter of personalities, a battle of egos. That is to say, at some level, *all conflict involves a threat to our identity.*

It bears repeating: conflict threatens our sense of self. It throws open to question our deeply held beliefs, our judgments and opinions, and the assumptions and stories we hold to be true. We feel in danger…like we have something to prove: *our selves!* We re-act automatically, falling back on our self proving mind ruts to protect and defend ourselves. Some people get angry and abusive. Some people get even. Some project their issues onto others and blame everyone for their unhappiness. Still others shut down emotionally and withdraw. All of these are examples of self proving thoughts and behaviors. They are ways we try to make ourselves feel safe. For the same reason, self proving often sounds self righteous because we need to present ourselves in the best possible light; to bolster and prop up our self-image. Most of all, at the deepest level, we want to regain control of the situation…so *I* can once again assume my rightful place as center of the universe. As we've said, *we re-act by self proving.*

Positional bargaining is perhaps the best example of the first Mental Lock in action and our re-active, self proving behavior. Positional bargaining involves a lot of posturing, wrangling, and ego-centric activity. It reflects the mind's dualistic and contrasting tendencies, creating two sides and two diametrically opposed positions. It presumes that with enough persuasion and skill, and the right argument, our view – *I* – will prevail. It is fueled by our identity:

> If you identify with a mental position, then if you are wrong, your mind-based sense of self is seriously threatened with annihilation…To be wrong is to die (Tolle, 1999, pp. 36).

Moreover, positional bargaining never forces us to question our assumptions; to wonder if, perhaps, our view is not *the* view of reality.

At The Zoo

And yet, we know no-one could possibly see the world as we do. Our perspective is uniquely our own. What we see, feel, and experience when we interact with the world is shaped by our entire history, our cultural and social conditioning, life experiences, and personal and universal proclivities; the very factors out of which we create a self. How we interpret events, perceive what needs to be done, understand what's happening and why – it's *our* reality, no-one else's.

Once, in a talk with Dr. Marshal Rosenberg, author of Non-Violent Communication–A Language for Life (2003), a woman described her distress at being accosted during an animal rights protest outside a zoo. She was passionate about her cause, to protect all animals, and convinced of the rightness of her position: she wanted all zoos closed because they were inhumane. She described her horror and disbelief when the zoo staff objected to her protest and asked her to leave.

"What did you want the zoo staff to do?" Dr. Rosenberg asked her.

"To help close down the zoo!" she said, indignantly, "They needed to see that they were part of the problem."

"Perhaps the zoo keepers felt they were protecting the animals from a worse fate," Dr. Rosenberg mused, "Did you ask them how they felt?"

When we re-act with self proving, we are ruled by our thoughts. We feel we have no choice but to protect and defend ourselves; our identity, that of our group, or our country. We are stuck in our assumptions and our repetitive behavior. We are so self-absorbed that we believe everyone sees the world as we do. When we self prove, we squander the possibilities.

AN AREA FOR FURTHER EXPLORATION

Third Chakra Consciousness

Our description of the self reflects a decidedly Eastern slant, which makes it more timeless than say, modern psychology. Eastern spiritual traditions, as with the ancient healing sciences, embody a longer horizon than most modern-day sciences. In Eastern traditions, such as Yoga, Tantra, and Kashmir Shaivism, *energy* is the organizing principle. Every thing in the Universe is made up of energy vibrating at a particular level. The energy of matter, for example, which is heavy and dense, vibrates at a low level.

One model of energy ascribed to by many Eastern traditions is that of the chakras. The chakras are energy centers of the subtle body, an *inner* body less tangible than the physical one. They are often portrayed as a series of wheels running up the human spine. There are seven chakras in total and each reflects a progressively higher level of awareness. The lower chakras, for example, are usually associated with security and stability, while the upper chakras are related to love, positive expression, inner peace, and Oneness (See Feuerstein, 2001, pp. 355).

When we self prove and focus too much on ourselves, we are said to be living in the third chakra, the "ego chakra". In the third chakra, we live as isolated individuals. We are separate and independent, acting as an "effective and competent force in the world"... functioning from a position of "power and control"...

and seeing the world from "ego-based Consciousness" (Nelson, 1996, pp. 312-3). We believe we are "masters of the universe." From the third chakra, we *are* the self. We live in our heads, believe things should go our way, and form mental ruts around our needs and desires. Yet the goal is not to eliminate the ego because the ego allows us to function effectively in the day-to-day world. The problem arises when we are dominated by the ego...when "me" becomes our primary or only frame of reference.

According to one author, "at this historical epoch, a majority of beings on earth have evolved to the third chakra" (ibid., pp. 312); but not beyond it. Eckhart Tolle reminds us, this "predominance of mind is no more than a stage in the evolution of consciousness" (Tolle, 1999, pp. 19). To move beyond this stage and the third chakra, we have to answer the question, "who are we, if not this self comprised of reasons, rationales, beliefs, opinions, judgments, and behaviors?"

Chapter 4

A Change of Mind

Self proving doesn't cause conflict. It's the belief the self is real – that we have an identity to protect and defend – that *causes* conflict. Self proving is what gets in the way of resolving conflict; it's the habitual ways we re-act when we feel threatened. Self proving is what makes us crazy when we try to talk with our partners; what compels us to interrupt another person to make our point; what forces us to cry out in frustration: "You can't communicate!" or "You're not listening!" In a conflict situation, we initially re-act by self proving; we often continue to fight over one another's self proving behavior.

To change how we deal with differences, we have to get *outside our selves.* We need to learn to talk, listen, and problem solve from a place beyond self proving; beyond the third chakra. While we don't want to eliminate differences, we can eliminate the ugliness that occurs when differences morph into full-blown conflict. Whenever we self prove, we re-act out of habit and fuel conflict's cycle of escalation. Re-activity closes off options. It constricts the breadth of possibilities...both mentally and physically.

The Physical Side of the Equation

Up until now, we've been talking about the mental side of conflict: how we shrink down into a self, an identity, mental ruts, and self proving. Conflict has a physical dimension as well. We all know that the body responds to any form of threat with the fight or flight response. When we're not under threat, the brain's neo-cortex and its many centers in the prefrontal areas, make sense of what we perceive and coordinate an organized and appropriate response. The prefrontal lobes are, however, also linked to the limbic brain, the seat of feelings, memories, and passion. As Daniel Goleman, author of <u>Emotional Intelligence</u>, explains, in a conflict situation, the brain receives strong signals of intense emotions such as anger, hate, and hurt which can create a kind of "neural static" that inhibits the prefrontal lobe from performing its assigned role (2006, pp. 27). Instead of a planned and balanced response, we re-act emotionally. We decide to fight or flee,

> And also, when to placate, persuade, seek sympathy, stonewall, provoke guilt, whine, put on a facade of bravado, be contemptuous – and so on (ibid., pp. 25).

In other words, *we self prove.* We simultaneously create the physical conditions that accompany such strong emotions: we have a rush of adrenaline, our body tenses, our shoulders grip, our face contorts, and every internal system is in a state of high alert. We re-act as we would to any form of stress.

Stress is what happens whenever we resist what is; when what's happening doesn't fit with what we want. We can feel stress before, during, and long after an argument. Under stress, the body releases stress hormones which suppress the functioning of the immune system, increase blood cholesterol levels, and leach calcium from our bones (See Benson 1992; Goleman and Gurin, 1993; and Kabat-Zinn, 1990). When stressed, we have a "lower threshold" for emotions like anger, which means that we tend to ignite more quickly (Goleman, 2006, pp. 60). When stress is coupled with other intense emotions like hostility and anger, it can damage organs like the heart and even impair the brain's ability to control the rate of heart beat. Yet, stress doesn't cause disease. The impact of stress depends on physical and mental factors: on the "type, frequency, duration and intensity" of the stressor; "the individual's appraisal" of the situation; his/her coping skills; and the individual's "set point" for stress (Ornstein and Sobel, 1991, pp. 213). That's why under similar circumstances, some people get sick and others do not.

Many of us think of stress as something that's done *to* us. It's "out there", someone or something causes us to feel stressful. Stress is not, however, an external condition. There is nothing inherently stressful for example, about being late for a meeting and having to sit at a dead stop in traffic while the next lane over moves right along. Rather, stress is a mental perception that takes place in the body. In fact, all emotions are mental perceptions that take place in the body. Consider the following situation:

> It is four o'clock; her daughter is dressed and ready to go, waiting in the hall for her Dad to show up. "I can't believe he's late again" she thinks, "why does he keep doing this to her? He's an insensitive bastard...but to her? Look at her, in her snow suit, all ready to go. He's such a jerk. He never thinks of anyone but himself. Just wait and see – he'll waltz in here like nothing's wrong, like he's totally innocent. That son-of-a-bitch. He has ruined my life and now I have to explain to her *again* that he's late...convince her that she wasn't forgotten, or second best. I have to..."

The stress seems to engulf her: her thoughts race and her body tenses. If someone were to ask, she'd say her ex-husband caused her stress. It is, in fact, the combined effect of her body and mind.

The same is true in an argument. Strong emotions like anger, hate, hurt, and fear resonate in the body/mind. They reinforce one another. Just as we form mental ruts in the mind that narrow our understanding and restrict the possibilities, we form "tension strategies or holding patterns" (Knaster, 1996, pp. 117) in the body which also restrict our experience. With repetition, they become what Mind/Body Medicine pioneer Wilhelm Reich calls "body armor". In a conflict situation, we habituate a certain way of standing, scrunch our faces, clench our jaw, and tense our shoulders:

> The character armor is your personal history embod-
> ied – all of your physical and emotional pains written
> on your body, their marks left in the form of cumulative
> restrictions of breathing and mobility (ibid.).

In other words, we constrict and lock into place. Re-activity shrinks our experience and our options.

How to Stop Self Proving

To begin to move beyond this place, we need to *interrupt the pattern of re-activity* – to create some space between what's happening and our re-action to it. This starts by **Noticing**. Noticing is the first technique for getting along in tough times. It's the first step towards greater awareness. Noticing isn't what we think. It isn't about becoming more alert and figuring out what caused the conflict. Noticing involves bringing our attention to a discussion at any point, and noticing ourselves *in the context* of the conversation.

We begin by concentrating our attention. In any argument, it's normal for our attention to be scattered. In addition to being offended, angry, worried, and flustered, we're planning what we'll say next, sizing up the other person, weighing our options, and anticipating the reaction we might get. So we begin by concentrating our attention as a single force and bringing that force to the conversation. It's as though another source of energy has entered the room. That energy is the power of noticing.

When we notice, we don't say or do anything. We don't judge or measure, or try to change anything. We don't scan the discussion for cues, assess the effectiveness of our argument, soften our approach, or test new tools. We don't challenge our re-actions or try to stop our thoughts. We simply stop and notice. We are both part of what's happening *and* apart from it. Without paying too much attention to any one thing, we notice the situation as a whole: our thoughts, our actions, our physical experience; the intensity of our emotions, how we're standing, how our posture shifts. We notice the other person, his facial expressions, how his body appears to feel. And we notice how we appear together. We notice as though we were *a fly on the wall.* We bring our whole attention to the conversation and slow things down. We become more present.

More Than Self Awareness

When we notice, the natural desire is to want *to do* something: we want to identify our patterns, label our triggers, or reflect on our behavior. This is called *self* awareness – we're trying to become more aware of ourselves. Quoting psychologist John Mayer of the University of New Hampshire, Daniel Goleman explains, "Self awareness...means being 'aware of both our mood and our thoughts about that mood'" (2006, pp. 47); it's where the "mind observes and investigates experience itself, including the emotions" (ibid., pp. 47). Another author puts it this way:

> [We are] cultivating our inner observer so that we become more aware of all parts of ourselves: physical, intellectual, and spiritual (LeBaron, 2002, pp. 160).

There is nothing wrong with self awareness – except that it

keeps the mind in charge. We analyze, investigate, identify, categorize, and otherwise give the mind something to do. We get distracted and lose focus. Self awareness also feeds the inclination to create a fabricated "entity" – a "second self", "observing ego," "Conscience", or witness – who observes what we do and might comment on its appropriateness. In self awareness, at some point, that witnessing presence must be released (See Epstein, 1995).

What we're talking about is not self awareness. It goes *beyond* self awareness. When we notice, we don't *do* anything. We simply notice. We are present. We are sowing the seeds of a more general awareness: the kind that slows the pace, relaxes the moment, and grounds us, as well as the people around us. Noticing of this sort interrupts the re-active flow, the force of habit. We are trying to interrupt the pattern rather than understand it. Most importantly, when we notice, we are not just noticing ourselves. We're noticing the entire context of the conversation. By widening our view, we begin the process of getting outside ourselves. The focus is greater than ourselves, it's the conversation and its context as a whole.

Taking Time to Notice

When we notice, we also breathe. Breathing addresses the physical dimension of conflict. We stop, focus our attention, and breathe. We take a long, deep breath. The breath brings us back into the body and calms us. The breath is uniquely qualified to do this because it links the body with the mind. If we want to see what our mind is doing, all we need to do is to look at our breath. In a conflict situation, when we feel afraid or anxious, our breath becomes short and constricted. When we feel relaxed, the breath deepens and our exhalation lengthens:

Respiration affects the right vagus nerve, which... controls the automatic nervous system and...regulates

the secretion of adrenaline, thyroxin, and other hormones, [all of which] play a major role in creating
one's emotional states" (Ajaya, 1983, pp. 196).

Unfortunately, according to Donna Farhi, an expert on
breathing, most of us don't breathe deeply. We are what Farhi
calls, "chest-breathers", breathing only in our upper chest
area (See Farhi, 1996). Moreover, we breathe through our
mouths:

> Humans come into this world as nose breathers. We
> are 'obligate nose breathers,' to be scientific...Mouth
> breathing is a learned response triggered by emergency
> stress (Douillard, 1994, pp. 151).

According to many Eastern traditions, the breath is more
than just air. When we breathe, we take in the oxygen we need
to survive and *prana*, a Sanskrit word for "life force" or the
energy "that holds things together" (Keller, 2001, pp. 8). The
life force is what animates us and brings consciousness to the
body. When we die, prana leaves the body which "becomes an
empty shell that quickly disintegrates" (ibid.).

So we notice and take a full, deep breath and exhale all our
air through the nose. With every inhalation, the body seems to
lift. With every exhalation, the inner body seems to lift as our
physical shell settles down. We feel more grounded; the mind
is quieter and we are present. Consider how a deep breath
might transform the following exchange:

Seller: "You're kidding, right? I sold you this house.
We went over every detail. I remember you
saying, 'you're a detail kind of guy.'"

Buyer: "I remember that. But that doesn't exempt
you from filling out the —"

Seller: "I remember standing in the basement and

saying, 'Yes, there had been standing water here once. But I had the problem resolved and it never happened again.' I remember telling you that. I am the most honest seller you're going to find. I do this for a living, this is my work."

Buyer: "I'm not saying anything about your hones-"

Seller: "The hell you're not. You didn't even bother to call me. You had your attorney write me a letter. This is *not* how two people do business."

Buyer: "The historical statement on the house never mentioned standing water. Or flooding. Now I've got this huge problem, an angry tenant, and a big expense. I don't forget things. And I definitely would have remembered this."

Seller: "And the letter suggested 'fraud.' Fraud! Do you have any idea how pissed off I was? I'm an established person in the community. I run a business here. I know people. I don't think you know who you're dealing with."

Buyer: "But the form –"

Seller: "The form said to note problems. This was not a problem. You're Joe Home Owner now; this is part of your job. Welcome to the world of tenants! You need to fix this, buddy, not me. I disclosed everything that was required. I'm not like some of those sellers; I went out of my way to show you every potential problem. I took extra time to–"

Buyer: "But you didn't write it d—"

Seller: "Look, buddy, I did exactly what was required of me. You..."

Now, stop the conversation right before the seller's last comment. Allow the seller to focus his attention and notice...

as though he was a fly on the wall. From there, he can see his tension, his hunched shoulders, and his seething face. He can see how anxious the buyer is, his clenched jaw, and the sweat running down his face. He notices they are both totally self-absorbed, inside their own heads and racing towards a confrontation. So he takes a deep breath. To his surprise, he notices the buyer does as well. The sound of a full, deep breath is contagious; others will follow suit. There is a momentary lull. The escalating tension seems suspended. The seller feels more grounded and relaxed, and he's able to say,

Seller:"Look, I feel like my reputation's on the line here, but how this was handled by your attorney was overkill for sure. I can't afford the solution you want, but I do remember the guy next door had a similar problem with his house and his is the same structure as yours. He had the roof drain re-routed away from the house and hasn't had a problem since. What do you say we each get two quotes to have that job done, meet for coffee and exchange them, and pick the best one – which might not be the lowest one – and I'll pay for that work. Then, if you still have a problem in say, four months of that work being done, we'll agree to try something else. What do you say?"

Awareness Comes

Noticing is a great deal harder than it appears. We first have to remember to notice and breathe, which is a matter of practice. When we first start to stop and notice, we're struck by how often we fall back on our self proving ways – how we forget to notice and let our thoughts take over as our body seizes up, our anger builds, and the conflict escalates.

Over time, awareness comes. Without much effort on our

part, we learn to recognize our re-active patterns: where perceptions and feelings feel stuck, assumptions appear locked in place, and behavior needs changing. Without having to analyze anything, we begin to name our re-actions, challenge the thoughts that sustain them, and consider alternatives. And then, we can try something altogether different! We can notice, take a deep breath, and do whatever we can other than what we would normally do – *anything*. Anything we can do other than reinforce the existing pattern will help to undermine it and lessen the mind rut. It will enable us to *respond*, instead of re-act.

In the midst of an argument, the possibilities are endless. We can change the venue, change our posture, or change the topic. We can say nothing or smile. We can set up ground rules; have the conversation in the dark, or laugh – at ourselves, at how quickly things get out of control. We can be transparent and admit how badly we feel, how insulted we were, or how worried we are over how our daughter makes sense of *either* parent being late. When we do something different, we make a little change in ourselves and **change begets change**: minor changes now, make future changes easier.

The Key

Whenever we feel threatened in a conflict situation, instead of re-acting with self proving, we notice, breathe, and try something different. The most important tool is noticing. When we stop to notice, we slow things down. We create space. Noticing broadens our experience, re-connects us with the present moment, and expands our range of options. It buys us a moment to switch off of automatic pilot and become more aware...to see that *all behavior is a choice*. We need to create enough space to make the choice a conscious one.

Through Noticing, we find **Compassion**. Compassion is the first key to getting along in tough times. It unlocks the assumption that everyone sees the world as we do and allows us to let it go. We first find Compassion when we notice just how badly we want to hold on to this assumption; how much we want to believe we are masters of the universe. We find it again when we learn just how hard it is to interrupt habit; how difficult it is to change the self proving that flows from this assumption. As we grow in awareness, we find Compassion for ourselves and for others. Compassion, noticing, breathing, and trying something different helps change our mind. It's essential. But it's not enough...at least not enough to change how we deal with differences.

AN AREA FOR FURTHER EXPLORATION

An Underlying Intelligence

There are many ways of looking at the world. We have already stated that in many Eastern traditions, energy is the organizing principle. Yoga, for example,

> Is anchored in two basic insights. The first is... that matter is only a low form of vibration of the same energy that exists in states of high velocity elsewhere. The second is that consciousness is not inevitably bound by matter but is inherently free (Feuerstein, 1996, pp. 127).

According to this view, the Universe begins as energy and *becomes* physical. In other words, energy or Consciousness comes first, and physical-ness comes later. This contrasts with the predominately mechanistic model in much of Western thought, where matter is primary and Consciousness is infused into the physical form.

Inherent in this alternative view is the idea of an all-embracing, overriding, organizing energy; an underlying intelligence that connects all things. According to Dr. Deepak Chopra,

> Centuries ago...there was universal agreement that the world is a seamless creation imbued with one intelligence, one creative design. Monotheism called the one reality God; India called it Brahman; China called it the Tao" (Chopra, 2004, pp. 22).

Chopra points to DNA, metamorphosis, and the way insects learn to fly as examples of this intelligence at work (ibid., pp. 22-24). Similarly, science argues that "space is not empty", that there are "invisible fields that exert visible influence" (Wheatley, 1992, pp. 48-50). There are, for example, the "unseen structures" of gravitational, electromagnetic, and quantum fields; the self-organizing qualities of fractals and chaotic attractors; chemical clocks, even biological functions such as menstrual cycles in groups of women, that suddenly come in sync (See Wheatley, 1992). According to Dr. Chopra,

> One reality isn't an idea – it is a doorway into a completely new way to participate in life...[where] Consciousness is the potential for all creation" (Chopra, 2004, pp. 33-4).

Section Three

Changing Your Relationships

Chapter 5

Relating to Others

We've been talking about ourselves, about changing our mind. We've seen that all conflict involves a threat to our identity and we react to that threat by self proving. We've learned to Notice as a way of interrupting the pattern of re-activity - - to slow the "automatic-ness" of habit and resist the urge to self prove. In relationships, another person enters the picture. Like any other situation, conflict in our relationships erupts whenever we feel threatened. But the problem is more than just a matter of the other person not seeing the world as we do. We also *assume we know.*

Born to Read People

Human beings are born and live in relationships; we are social by nature. Time and time again, research has confirmed the critical importance of the caregiver-infant relationship. Early research found, for example, when infants enter the world, they are already intimately linked with their environment:

> Infants are found to reliably turn their heads towards the smell of their mother's milk versus the milk of another...(MacFarlane, 1975); infants have been found to have a preference for the human voice versus other sounds...(Friedlander, 1970); and infant looking patterns have revealed their preference for looking at faces rather than other visual stimuli (Franz,

> 1963)...[Infants] are active and aware from the start, purposely engaged in the business of relating to the environment (Firman and Gila, 1997, pp. 30-31).

These and related studies have shown that babies grow and evolve in the context of a nurturing and enmeshed relationship with their caregiver, and without it, they can develop abnormalities. Through this connection, babies form cognitive skills, learn about emotions and how to regulate them, and discover how to be with others (See Gaussen, 2000, pp. 123-132). They learn how to "read" other people, how to make sense of another person's behavior:

> This represents a peculiar type of intelligence related to understanding mental states such as desires, intentions and beliefs from the other's bodily presence: face, posture and sound (Varela, 2000, pp. 80).

More recent research is shedding new light on the science behind our relationships. In Daniel Goleman's follow-up book, Social Intelligence, he examines what recent advances in the field of Social Neurology tell us about how we relate to one another. Once again, this research verifies the key role of the caregiver, confirming that the "parent-child loop" is *the* critical pathway for parents to teach their children how to relate to others. In this relationship, children learn:

> How to pace an interaction, how to engage in conversation, how to tune in to the other person's feelings, and how to manage your own feelings...These essential lessons lay the foundations for a competent social life (Goleman, 2006, pp. 164).

Goleman suggests that Social Intelligence is comprised of two parts: being socially aware and being socially able. He argues that both are linked to new findings about how the brain helps us "read" people and situations. One such finding involves a type of brain cell known as mirror neurons. Mirror neurons impulsively make us mimic the emotions or actions we see in someone else: "we 'feel' the other in the broadest sense", sensing the other person's emotions as if we were experiencing them ourselves (ibid., pp. 42). He also points to a new class of neurons called spindle cells. Spindle cells help us understand a social situation and make snap decisions to respond to it accordingly. Some scientists even theorize that spindle cells might explain why some people are more sensitive and socially adept than others (ibid., pp. 65-69).

Most of us assume we're pretty good at reading people. Goleman warns us though: our ability to read people and situations depends on how attentive we are. He cautions that under stress, as in a conflict situation, the social cues we rely on don't register as effectively and our accuracy falters. In other words, instead of being aware and able, we "personalize" what's happening.

Framing the Experience

Mirror neurons and spindle cells aside, our experience of emotions is still our own and one way we put our personal stamp on it is through "framing." Frames are "interpretive lenses" or "shortcuts" we use to help "make sense of complex situations" (Shmueli, Elliot, and Kaufman, 2006, pp. 208). They allow us to:

> Name situations...identify and interpret... and communicate our interpretations to others... [They] help us reduce information overload... organize phenomenon... [and give] meaning... to unfolding events (ibid.).

Frames help us manage the world around us. They let us take information in, process and explain it, and convey that explanation to others. The problem with framing and its particular relevance to conflict is that we use frames to *filter* information. Through framing, we make sense of situations "in ways internally consistent with our worldviews" (ibid.). We filter out what we don't want to hear or what doesn't support our argument, and emphasize what does. In other words, through frames, we shape our experience of reality.

Doctors, for example, often think in terms of frames. As the patient is describing his/her list of symptoms, the doctor immediately starts to frame a diagnosis. He/she categorizes the symptoms and reaches a conclusion. Fortunately, that conclusion is usually correct. However, if the frame occurs too early in the discussion, or takes hold too rigidly, it can lead to an incorrect diagnosis. The following exchange provides an example of a couple sharing a difficult conversation, each from within their own set of frames:

Wife: "Okay, so, this isn't working for you. I under-stand. *I get it.* I agree we've had some problems. Things haven't been great...for a while, so you say...I guess. So how do we make it better, how do we turn things around?"

Husband: "You're not hearing me. I can't live like this anymore. I can't keep doing this. I don't want to hurt you, but this isn't working for me."

Wife: "I *did* hear you, but how can we make it work? It worked once, for a long time. We've got dreams together, we've got a future together, and we've got *kids!* We've got family, history, and friends. Families stay together. Families don't give up on one another. Divorce is not a word in this family. So what do we need to do? Do we need to spend more time together? More alone time? Should we go away on holiday? What do you want to do?"

Husband: "You're right. We need to do what's best for everyone."

Wife:"That's right; we need to do this together. We need to tackle this together. There's a lot of love here."

Husband: "But there's not enough left to continue as we are..."

Wife: "I understand that. Things have got to change. I'm agreeing with you, for Christ's sake. Wait... What are you saying? Are you saying...that...you don't love me?"

Husband: "I'll always love you, the times we had. There will always be love here..."

This is a rather classic, and painful, case of framing. Throughout the conversation, her frame is, "how do we make this work," while he's saying, "its over," in a way he understands and hopes will minimize her pain. As we can see, the "selective simplification" that happens in framing can lead to "sharply different interpretations of events" (ibid.). Frames also tend to be self-reinforcing because they "color" new information so it conforms to our frames.

Frames are mind ruts. They are re-active patterns that support self proving. They are another example of how anger and conflict breed more of the same, and escalate out of control. Frames also give us a taste of just how far the self will go when it feels threatened: it will bend reality to make it fit. Most importantly, frames restrict available options; they contract the options down to those in keeping with our frames.

The Second Mental Lock

Arguments are fast-paced, rife with emotions, hard-hitting, and spiral quickly out of control. To try to manage this stress, we take our already hamstrung ability to read people and combine it with our distorted personal frames...and then we step over a line. We engage the second Mental Lock: **we assume we know.**

Recall that a Mental Lock is an unconscious belief that helps props up our self and identity, which makes it incredibly powerful; they keep us stuck in one place and lock out what really matters. The second Mental Lock is we assume we know – what another person is saying, how they feel, and what they need. We go beyond interpreting events and reading emotions, and we believe we know. This wholesale assumption shuts down the conversation and closes off any chance of understanding...because we already know. What makes matters worse, very often, *we're wrong.*

A landlord and tenant sit down to have a conversation about a recurring problem:

Landlord: "You've got to curb your dog. It's that simp–"

Tenant: "Curb my dog? Are you out of your mind, we live in the middle of nowhere. There's no curb here."

Landlord: "Look, I have tried to work with you. I've–"

Tenant: "Tried to work. Please tell me what that means. I rented this place from your Dad. He said dogs were fine. I've lived here without incident for seven years. There's never been a problem. I live here quietly –"

Landlord: "Quietly? You have those wild parties over there...with all those men!"

Tenant: "Oh, please. *How* is this relevant? And besides, there's only one man and we're not wild by any standard. Not even yours."

Landlord: "And what is *that* supposed to mean? You think you're so smart with all those degrees all over your walls – *my* walls – but I work for the town. I hold a very respectable job. I make a lot of money."

Tenant: "Yeah, okay, whatever. I have trained the dog, as you know, to go only in the back field. It was difficult bu–"

Landlord: "The dog is peeing on my lawn!"

Tenant: "You want the dog *to pee* in a particular place? Are you crazy? There's fifteen acres of lawn out here! What should I do, pick her up, walk a half mile to the field, and then set her down to pee? We've lived here for *seven years*. I can't train the dog to pee in a particular place. She's older than you are!"

Landlord: "Stop getting so worked up. You've got to learn to calm down."

Tenant: "*I am not worked up.* I am being very patient with you. I think you're being unreasonable."

Landlord: "You've had family problems, haven't you? I think your mother wore the pants in your family, that's what I think. And now you have trouble with constructive criticism."

Tenant: "What, did you hear that big word at work...at your *respectable* job? Besides, what I have difficulty with is none of your business. I am a professional person, and fully in control of my emo–"

Landlord: "*That dog* is ruining my lawn. I'm in charge now and what I say goes. What my Dad said when he was landlord is no longer relevant."

Tenant: "Your Dad was reasonable. He liked the idea that he had an established, professional person living here–"

Landlord: "Professional, my ass. I make more money than you. You may think you're important, but with all those men at your place, you should get some counseling. Ha! That's it! You're not a professional, you need *professional help!*"

Tenant: "What I need is —"

Landlord: "Counseling! You need counseling. The problem is that you don't know how to be a good tenant. You don't respect other people's things. You need to learn to control your attitude."

Tenant: "– legal advice, was what I was going to say. You've lost all sense of reason here."

Landlord: "Go ahead, get a lawyer. But if you go back and wreck the place in the meantime, I will sue your ass so fast; your head will sp–"

Tenant: "You know I would never do that. What is the matter with you? I think you've got some kind of psychological problem or something. I've always gotten along with everyone here. Your wife is lovely and –"

Landlord: "Don't you bring my wife into this. Don't you dare. She's a good woman. She knows her place. She doesn't need any of your strange ideas. *I'm* the man of *my* house –"

Tenant: "Oh, get over yourself. You're *a* man *in a* house, that's about it. Besides, this is about the dog."

Landlord: "That's right and you need to learn to respect *my* property. Or, get rid of the dog."

Tenant: "I'm not getting rid of the dog. I–"

Landlord: "*And* you need to replace the refrigerator you've ruined. You put contact paper on it! It looks like crap."

Tenant: "Your Dad said it was a great idea to use contact paper to help cover *the rust* that's all over it! The frig barely works, and I'm not sure what the town will say when they find out your "hot" water tank is *above* ground – *outside the house!* I didn't have hot water half the winter!"

Landlord: "That's it. *You* need to go. You're trouble."

Tenant: "I am not trouble. I'm a responsible adult. I don't have to live up to your expectations. Who the hell do you think you are? I have rights, here. I'll drag your ass into court. I'll show you–"

Landlord: "Move out. That's it. You, young lady, are evicted. And I'm using your deposit to find another tenant because you won't curb your dog."

Tenant: "Now I definitely need some –"

Landlord: "Counseling! You're a libber! That's your problem. You're one of those women who got educated and now you think your shit doesn't stink. Well, let me tell you, I know women like you. They boss you around and make you feel small. I..."

This is a pretty typical argument between two people – identities are at stake and there is an ample supply of self proving. While the problem appears to be about the dog, it runs far deeper than that. They both assume they know – a lot!

How "We Assume We Know"

There are many telltale signs we've locked down, assuming we know what the other person is saying, how they feel, and what they need. Some are pretty obvious:

- <u>We tell them</u>. Often in confrontations, we tell people what they need, as in the above case, "You need counseling!" Statements such as you need to "get your head examined", "go to parenting classes," "learn to deal with criticism," "grow up", "get over it", "get a hold of yourself", etc., are all assumptions – we think we know what the other person needs.

- <u>We finish their sentences</u>. In couples and other long-term relationships, one person often completes the other's sentences. If the parties are well-attuned, he/she can be very accurate. In an argument, however, the practice can be sarcastic, controlling, and just plain wrong.

- <u>We "therapize"</u>. When we therapize, we slip into our counseling mode and psychoanalyze the other person. The landlord was "therapizing" when he suggested the tenant had family issues. Similarly, couples bring up one another's alcohol or substance abuse, driving record, run-ins with the police, time spent in jail, etc., when they therapize. Once this kind of information is public knowledge, it becomes fair game in an argument.

- <u>We "mind-read"</u>. When we mind-read, we tell the other person what he/she's thinking. We say such things as: "You know I would never be that way", "You're just doing this to hurt me", "You thought I was going to take this forever", "You never listen", and similar statements. Mind-reading often includes the words, "always" or "never", and generally starts with "You".

- <u>We "fix it"</u>. Another telltale sign that "we assume we know" is when we rush to fix things. Instead of listening, we assume we already know what the problem is and how to fix it. Fixing the problem can be an indirect attempt to control the conversation, avoid a confrontation, or quickly restore the status quo. The "fixer" may also rationalize that by making an effort, he or she is blameless.

There are other, more subtle ways we assume we know. One indicator is the number of <u>tangential issues</u> that clutter the conversation. In the above example, the landlord mentions men and wild parties, the contact paper on the refrigerator, and the deposit, while the tenant brings up his father and wife, the hot water heater, and the need for legal advice. Tangential issues can sometimes mean a lot has been bottled up that is now coming up for discussion. They can also be used tactically as deliberate distractions. As is often the case, tangential issues prove our conclusions; we use them to confirm what we already know to be true.

One final way we assume we know is through what authors Kolb and Williams call the "<u>shadow negotiation</u>" (Kolb and Williams, 2003). The shadow negotiation is an exchange that occurs slightly beneath the surface of what's being discussed. As opposed to issues, the shadow negotiation is about the relationship itself and "relational" concerns: how people treat one another, the balance of power, how willing parties are to cooperate, and how open and honest they feel they can be (See Kolb and Williams, 2003). According to these authors, "Because the root of the conversation remains hidden or disguised, the underlying issues cannot be addressed" (ibid., pp. 235). In the above case, the shadow conversation is about power. Left unexamined, the landlord will write the tenant off as yet another "one of those libbers", and she will see him as a macho pig. Deep down, they both want respect.

You Need to...

In the heat of an argument, the second Mental Lock often sounds like this: "I know what you need. You need *to change.*" When the second Lock is engaged, we give meaning to what another person says or does based on ***what makes sense to us***. It's a form of self proving: we focus on the flaws and the faults of the other person as a way to absolve and validate ourselves. We crawl back into the third chakra and become self-absorbed. We stop Noticing, don't take a deep breath, and forget to try something new to undo a well-worn path. We re-act.

Most importantly, when we assume we know, *we discount the other person.* We de-value what they bring to the conversation and fail to treat them like a credible and capable person in their own right. By assuming we know, we presume they don't...at least not as well as we do. And we deliver that message every time we assume we know. We lose touch with Compassion, with the capacity to feel.

AN AREA FOR FURTHER EXPLORATION

A Process of Universal Contraction

Kashmir Shaivism is an Eastern tradition gaining popularity as a result of its links to Yoga and Yoga Philosophy. According to Kashmir Shaivism, there is a universal tendency towards contraction. Consciousness is said to begin as pure energy, a sense of being or "am-ness". It is, however, by nature, playful and inquisitive, and therefore seeks to manifest as a way to experience itself. In other words, without form, Consciousness has no experience. Consciousness assumes the many forms we know to exist in the Universe in order to experience what it's like *to feel.* From that point forward, Consciousness is said to contract (See Shantananda, 2003).

The process of contraction occurs in a series of stages. From the initial feeling of "am-ness", the Universe differentiates into two equal experiences: the feeling of "I" and of "am". Taken together, this next stage forms the experience of "I am", where "I" and "am" are evenly weighted; it is neither "*I* am", nor "I *am.*" From there, the cosmic laws take form to organize the universe, giving rise to time, space, illusion, and desire. Intelligence and a sense of identity also come into being, as does the power of perception and action. In the next series of contractions, Consciousness creates the capacity to feel and sensations to experience (ibid., pp. 386; See also Sutras 3, 4, and 5).

According to many Eastern traditions, man is a microcosm of the Universe, meaning that this contraction occurs on both a universal and an individual plane. As energy contracts on a universal scale to create the cosmic laws, a sense of identity, and ultimately, the sensations of sound, touch, sight, taste and smell, the same happens in man. Energy contracts to form an intellect, ego, and ultimately, the physical receptors to experience sensations: our ears, skin, eyes, tongue, and nose. We contract from pure energy to a particular kind of person, a particular body type, a unique temperament, a solidified self. This explains why people are so very much the same and, at the same time, so unique. Our source, as pure energy, also ensures we are imbued with a sense of inner wisdom – of pure potential – which we can tap into and cultivate at any time.

Chapter 6

Being with "Family"

Our intimate relationships are a confluence of "mosts". They are our most important relationships; with the people we love the most – family, friends, siblings, parents, and partners. These are the people who showed us how to be in relationship and how to be ourselves; who give us a sense of belonging and a secure base. Our intimate relationships tend to be our most challenging relationships, where our identity feels most at stake. Family mind ruts are the easiest ruts to fall back into, even after years of separation. The frames we form of our intimates are more rigid and difficult to change: we share a common history, know the same people, and lived the same stories. With "family", we are especially prone to re-act to one another's self proving – because they are the ones who taught us how to self prove in the first place.

Not surprisingly, in our intimate relationships, we assume we know the most as well. We assume we know who these people are and who they want to be; their foibles, faults, and their pain. We assume we know what they want, what makes them tick, and what they need and desire. As in any other situation, very often, we're wrong...which can make our intimate relationships among the most argumentative and conflict-laden. Yet, rarely, do we move beyond our assumptions and deal with what hurts. When conflict involves "family", we may say the issue's been resolved, but the hurt often remains.

The Dance of Conflict

In an examination of couples, Drs. Clifford Notarius and Howard Markman, authors of <u>We Can Work It Out</u>, identified four basic styles of conflict which are generally applicable to all intimate relationships. They are pursuers, withdrawers, boilers, and steamers (See Notarius and Markman, 1993).

Pursuers and withdrawers (or avoiders) often come as a pair. Pursuers can't leave a problem alone. They need to talk about it, often at length, and will do whatever is takes to get the problem out on the table. Avoiders don't want to talk about it. They shy away from every kind of confrontation and if pursued, will ignore the problem and hope it goes away. Avoiders may leave the room, change the topic, or suggest they discuss the matter later and then forget about it. According to these authors, women are more often pursuers and men, avoiders. When paired together, they're called "vicious cyclers" (ibid., pp. 39).

When both parties are pursuers and tend to attack each other relentlessly, they're called "explosive boilers". Explosive boilers are "very good at speaking their minds, but they are not as good at listening" (ibid.). In an argument, they frequently talk over one another and jump randomly from topic to topic. Explosive boilers need very little provocation, their arguments escalate rapidly, and they are often ruthless in their attacks. Under the right circumstances, explosive boilers can resort to violence.

"Silent steamers" would rather withdraw than confront a problem; they're "stewers". Silent steamers stew over a problem, repeatedly mulling it over in their heads. They will often talk to anyone who will listen – except the person directly involved – about every detail of the situation, and readily seek out the advice and opinions of friends, family, co-workers, etc. Silent steamers prefer to "stew about how wronged they feel and how unjustly they are being treated" (ibid., pp. 40), than take corrective action.

Since none of these destructive styles actually help resolve conflict, we tend to argue about the same problems again and again. In time, "if these patterns become ingrained, [we become] *controlled* by [them]" (ibid., pp. 38). We begin to perform a well-rehearsed dance: we each assume we know what the problem is and how the other person needs to change to fix it.

The Emotions We Feel

When intimate partners fight, we fight dirty – we bring up the pain! We hit where it hurts and we're good at it because we taught one another how. We're not afraid to bring up the bulimia, the drunken stupor, the affair, the bi-polar brother-in-law, or the history of family violence. Our feelings spew out, flying in every direction in an angry tirade. Pursuers will incessantly ask, "What are you feeling?", only to stop listening if, by chance, the avoider has a response. Boilers never feel safe enough to talk honestly about their feelings, so they scream instead. And steamers stay angry, looking for proof they've been wronged long after the argument has ended. Regardless of our particular style of conflict, feelings seldom get the attention they need.

Emotions are at the heart of every conflict and are what matter most in our intimate relationships. When important feelings are left unaddressed, they don't go away. They accumulate and fester. They find a place to hide in the mind-body and become fodder for a future argument; part of our litany of unresolved hurts. For many of us, feelings are just too scary to express or receive from others. We simply don't have the tools for dealing with them. In fact, we sometimes struggle to understand what feelings even are.

Consider the following statements and ask yourself, whether or not they express feelings:
- I feel that you should know better.
- I feel inadequate.
- When you don't greet me, I feel neglected.
- I feel you don't love me.

- – You're disgusting.
- – I'm worthless.

This exercise is adapted from Dr. Marshal Rosenberg's <u>Non-violent Communication - A Language of Life</u> (See Rosenberg, 2003), and it's not as easy as it looks. Dr. Rosenberg asserts that *none* of these are a true expression of feelings. According to Rosenberg, words like inadequate, worthless, and neglected do not capture feelings at all, and the other statements are simply accusations. He suggests that many of the words we normally associate with feelings – such as being ignored, patronized, pressured, threatened, manipulated, overworked, taken for granted, or unwanted – are not feelings either. Rather, they are our *interpretation* of the actions or intent of others (ibid., pp. 43).

Since feelings are part of every discussion and every argument as well, Rosenberg suggests we need to build a vocabulary for feelings. In contrast to the above, he uses words like alive, amazed, contented, curious, engrossed, free, joyous, refreshed, surprised, and tender, for situations when our needs are being met; and anxious, ashamed, discouraged, fidgety, impatient, mad, nervous and scared, to express when they are not. He cautions to always use the phrase, "I feel ____," and *not*, "I feel that you ____."

When we start to label our feelings, it becomes harder to blame the other person for how we feel; and harder still, to assume we know. For example, the statement, "You think this marriage was a complete waste. Five years and it means nothing to you", is an assumption; we're mind-reading. It accuses the other person and will likely trigger more anger, not less. In contrast, the statement, "I feel heart-broken...and scared", expresses a feeling; it doesn't *assume* anything and as a result, invites discussion. When we name our feelings, we own them. We can start to clear our mind of the myriad assumptions that clutter it...so we can actually begin to hear.

Beginning to Hear

Like interrupting a habit, hearing starts with Noticing. When we Notice, we don't *do* anything. We simply Notice. We take a deep breath, slow the pace, relax the moment, and find the ground. We become aware that our mind is too full, that we long for spaciousness...what some spiritual traditions call "Beginner's Mind", or "Don't Know Mind." According to Zen Master Shunryu Suzuki, author of Zen Mind, Beginner's Mind, "The mind of a beginner is empty, free of the habits of the expert" (Suzuki, 1997, pp.13-14). He explains,

> Usually when you listen...you hear it as a kind of echo of yourself. You are actually listening to your own opinion...When you listen to someone, you should give up all your preconceived ideas and your subjective opinions; you should just listen to him, just observe what his way is (ibid., pp. 89).

A Beginner's Mind doesn't know. More importantly, it *doesn't need* to know. This is one of the primary tools of mediation. A good mediator will never offer a solution; he/she will not recommend a particular course of action. By not needing to know the answer, the mediator can be fully present; his/her identity is not involved. In fact, Transformative mediators take this idea a step further: they don't need to understand the problem being discussed in the mediation session. Rather than try to comprehend the specific issue, they trust the parties know their situation best and they follow the parties' lead (See Bush and Folger, 2005).

With a Beginner's Mind, we get comfortable *not knowing*. It opens us up to a different kind of knowing that is not ego-based, not so hard-and-fast. A Beginner's Mind is a spacious mind. It's a safe place for expressing and experiencing emotions because it doesn't judge, strategize, or analyze. As soon as we adopt a Beginner's Mind, feelings can be heard.

Feeling Heard

Hearing is a two step process: it requires space for speaking and space for understanding. This means that in order to hear, we must create enough space for the other person to talk, and then work until *they* are convinced we understand what's been said. This is the second technique for getting along in tough times: **We Reflect *First*.** It's the next step towards greater awareness.

Reflecting *first* applies to feelings and everything else that's said or done in an attempt to deal with differences. We reflect from the moment the conversation begins, and especially at the slightest inkling of tension. We *lead* with it. We reflect *first*. Instead of going back inside and pulling out what we assume we know, we reflect *first*:

- "So, it sounds like you're really upset about last night, and you want me to call when I'm late so you know I'm safe, is that it?";
- "You're saying my bringing up your binge drinking was hurtful, and that you wish I hadn't done it in front of your family, is that right?";
- "So you think I want to relocate to take the kids away from you. Is that what you're saying?"

We listen and create space for the other person to speak; we Notice, breathe, and slow the pace. We adopt a Beginner's Mind and reflect *first*. And then we ask, "Is that correct"?

Not Active Listening

Reflecting *first* is not the same as active listening. Tool #5 in Chapter One recommends active listening. It suggests we restate what's been said to ensure we've heard it correctly. Reflecting *first* is more than simply confirming we've heard what was said. When we reflect *first*, we force ourselves to listen *before* we feel heard. We create a safe space for the other person to talk, even though we may have a lot to say. We Notice, center ourselves, and give the other person the floor. Moreover, we invite and encourage them to say *more*. We ask them to elaborate, share their emotions, and tell their story, if they want to. We "lean into emotions", or anything else that needs to be given a voice.

When we reflect *first*, we offer the other person a chance to go deeper; to go beyond interests to the needs, feelings, and intentions which drive them – if they want to. We do so without making any assumptions: we don't finish their sentences, read minds, psychoanalyze the past, regurgitate a laundry list of unresolved tangential hurts, or try to hide what's really at stake. We let our assumptions fall away and approach what's said with curiosity. We keep the conversation going until the other person feels heard; until we reflect *first* and they say, "That's it!"

Reflect *First*

So perhaps you're wondering, "What is it that I reflect?" The answer is, whatever you see or hear or feel. Reflection has many uses and variations. It can help un-bundle loaded concepts, like "respect" or "communication". We might say, "You've mentioned that several times. What do you mean when you say you 'need respect'?" We can use reflection when the other person falls silent and we're not sure what's going on: "So, you're sitting there with your arms crossed and sighing. You seem really angry, like everybody's against you. Is that how you feel?" Reflection can also help us be more transparent with our own needs and feelings. Recall the husband in one of our first arguments who was having difficulty over the deed to his house. If he had reflected *first*, he might have said, "Look, it seems like this deed thing is really important to you, and I'll be honest, I don't get it. You never mentioned it before we got married. Can you clue me in on this one?"

Reflecting *first* helps defuse the situation, especially potentially explosive ones. Consider the following examples:

Example #1.

Co-Parent 1: "You cut my visitation."

Co-Parent 2: "I eliminated your overnight visits *temporarily*. You haven't exactly shown yourself to be a responsible parent. Our son had just enough medication to get him through his last visit at your house and he came home with 5 pills left over. He has a mental disorder. He needs to take his medication. You may not want to admit it but this is serious stuf–"

Co-Parent 1: "Oh, this old sob story... 'he has a disorder, he needs to be medicated.' You need a new excuse, princess. But I've gotcha this time. I'm gonna be all over you in court. Your crazy husband threatened our son and I've got it on tape! You're going to lose this one. You think you've got it nailed, but it is over."

At this point, Co-Parent 2 could take a deep breath and Notice. She could adopt a Beginner's Mind and elect not to engage in the dance. She could reflect *first* by saying: "So you don't feel that this disorder is real and he needs medication, is that what you're saying?" or, "You're saying that you've got my husband threatening our son on tape and you want to take that tape into court. Is that correct?" or, "So you think the only way to resolve the visitation problem is by going to court. Is that right?"

Example #2.

Father: "You're in no position to get married. You can't even take care of yourself. You're too young. You don't have a job. And he's a loser. Why would you even consider marrying this guy?"

Daughter: "You seem to know an awful lot from meeting him once. And I can take care of myself just fine, thank you very–"

Father: "Yeah, right. So answer this: *how* do you take care of yourself? Go ahead. Answer me. You seem to have all the answers."

Daughter: "I eat. Are you happy now? That's why I weigh two hundred pounds! I self soothe, as you call it. Does that make you feel any better Dad? Does it?"

The Father could pause and Notice. He could take the entire situation in, Notice his tension and her pain, and reflect *first*: "So, you think this whole thing is about your weight?" Or, "I guess that self soothe speech I gave really hurt, am I right?" Or, "So, you think getting married will help you take better care of yourself. Is that what you're saying?"

Example 3.

After a lengthy discussion, back-and-forth, the Wife decides to cut to the chase and settle the matter once and for all:

Wife: "So I've made my offer. I've put my cards on the table. Now it's up to you. You have to decide. Do you want to fix this problem or make it worse? Are you going to try what I suggest and work this out, or what?"

The Husband could Notice, breathe, and try something altogether different. He could say, "So...you're suggesting the only way to resolve this problem is for me to agree with you. Yes?" At that point, chances are, both people would smile. Reflecting *first* helps both partners get outside themselves. It empties the mind and expands the possibilities.

The Key

Reflect *first* doesn't suddenly transform our intimate partners into cooperative allies. Even with Reflect *first*, arguments will wax and wane. It does help mitigate the ugliness that's common when intimate partners and family members fight.

It also helps ensure we don't teach our kids to fight the same way – to repeat when they've learned in the parent-child loop. Reflect *first* expands awareness. When we Notice, breathe, and reflect *first*, we're able to get past the steady stream of thoughts and realize that ***all behavior is functional***...it makes sense, even if we don't understand it. In other words, we find forgiveness.

Forgiveness is the second key to getting along in tough times. We learn to forgive ourselves for assuming we know; and for holding on so tightly. So, too, we learn to forgive others. In a book about working with angry couples, the authors describe what they call "the disempowered parent." The disempowered parent is a partner "who has the least power" in the relationship and develops "problem behaviors" as a way of "equalizing" the power base (Gaulier, Price, and Windell, 2007, pp. 102 [citing Madanes, 1981]). This partner is "angry about nearly everything" and engages in every conceivable form of dysfunctional behavior to inconvenience, manipulate, and outright offend the other partner (ibid., pp. 102-3). To their surprise, these authors found that reprimanding such a person, through the courts or otherwise, only made the situation worse. He or she behaved more aggressively. What changed this person's behavior was for the mediator to "wonder with both parties whether the co-parent [had] any redeeming value", and to demonstrate faith in the disempowered parent (ibid., pp. 106-7). What worked was Compassion and Forgiveness.

Forgiveness unlocks the need to assume we know. We see it as just another form of resistance and we're able to let it go. We understand that everyone says and does something for a reason, and that it's not our job to figure it out why. Actually, it's quite a relief.

AN AREA FOR FURTHER EXPLORATION

Contracting Further Still

Ayurveda is an ancient Indian science of wellness dating back to 1000 BC. According to this tradition, in the process of universal contraction, five great elements are created. The great elements are ether, air, fire, water, and earth, and they comprise every thing in the Universe. The elements, in turn, combine to form three vital energies: Vata, Pitta, and Kapha. Vata is the combination of ether and air, Pitta of fire and water, and Kapha of water and earth.

The vital energies also represent "body types" or constitutions. According to Ayurveda, every human being has all three energies in a unique proportion. Some people are predominately one energy – Vata, Pitta, or Kapha; others are a combination – Vata-Pitta, Pitta-Kapha, or Vata-Kapha (for a body type test, or additional information, see Lad, 1996 or Morrison, 1995):

- Vatas have a nervous, spacious energy. They tend to be tall or very short, thin and bony, have trouble maintaining their weight, and have dry skin. Vatas love change and excitement, have trouble sitting still, are inclined towards worry and nervousness. Vatas enjoy a lot of activity, are restless, and tend to have low endurance. They are especially sensitive to sound and touch.

- Pittas have a fiery, hot energy. They tend to be medium height and weight, have a ruddy complexion, often thinning hair and solid appetite. Pittas have a piercing intelligence, are often opinionated and hot-headed, and are sensitive to heat, sunlight, and fire. For Pittas, sight or seeing is the sensation they respond to most.

- Kaphas have a slow, solid energy. They tend to be short and gain weight easily. They have lustrous hair, beautiful voices, thick skin, and are sensitive to cold and damp. Kaphas often struggle with change, prefer leisure to heated exercise, and have a content, conservative temperament. Kaphas are most sensitive to the sensations of taste and smell (See Frawley, 1996, pp. 24-25).

According to this tradition, there are "master forms" of Vata, Pitta, and Kapha as well, "which keep us healthy and free of disease" (ibid., pp. 25). The master forms derive from the nutrients we eat and "are fed by the impressions we take in from the senses" (ibid., pp. 26). Thus, in Ayurveda, everything we experience leaves an energetic imprint on us – physically, mentally, and emotionally...just as we do on others.

Chapter 7

A New Definition of Help

To release the need to know requires a more enlightened definition of help. When we assume we know, "helping" is an action; it's something we do *for* someone else. We assume we know on their behalf and act accordingly based on what makes sense to us. To get along in tough times, helping means something else: it means being present.

Being present for another person in a conversation is a very special skill. Too often we believe that communication is just a matter of getting our point across. We speak to someone as though they're the mark and we need to nail the sale; or we talk at them and tell them what to do. Talking with someone is different. There are *two* people involved; two equally competent people, each knowing their situation best. We appreciate and value what the other person brings to the conversation. We're not there to help them: they don't need our help and invariably, they don't want it either. Besides, what we think may be way off the mark.

The fact is most people just want to talk. They want to talk first and feel heard, and then, they might be willing to listen. This requires moving outside our selves and our need to know, and simply being present: no opinions, no advice, and no assumptions. No mind-reading, no psychoanalyzing, and no preaching. This is the hallmark of Transformative Mediation: the belief that each person is capable and knows his/her own situation best (See Bush and Folger, 2002). Yet the techniques of Noticing and Reflect *first* suggest we can solve *our own* problems, without relying on outside intervention. We trust that between the two of us, we have what we need. A conversation becomes a connection, an exchange: a means to discover different ways of moving forward.

In this chapter, we will use an example to pull together the techniques we've discussed so far, and offer some additional tools that expand our capacity to help without doing. Chapter Eight returns to specific kinds of relationships, focusing on those in the workplace.

The Will – Take 1

Using the body typology presented at the close of the last chapter, the following case study involves a Pitta Daughter, high strung and under a lot of stress, and a Vata Mother, who feels anxious about many things:

Mother: "I want to talk with you about the–"

Daughter: "The will. I know, I know. You've been hinting about it for weeks. Mom, just let it go. I know you're worried about the finances but there's no reason to discuss it. I'm sure you handled it just as you want. And we'll find out about it when the time comes."

Mother: "But, I'm afraid it will upset you. So I want to talk about it now."

Daughter: "Mom, I've got a lot going on right now. It's not the best time. And I really don't want to know, to be honest with you."

Mother: "This is your way. It's always been your way. You ignore things in the hopes they'll go away, but I won't let you do it to me this time. I always let you win. Dad always said you were like this."

Daughter: "Pray tell me, which *dad* are we talking about? There were so many loving, caring people you brought home and forced us to—"

Mother: "– make part of our family. *Try* to stay focused, will you? I've decided to sell the house and split the money between you and your brother."

Daughter: "My brother. My brother. You're kidding, right? The brother who's two thousand miles away? The brother who's never been here to help with anything? The brother who sends little barbs over the phone, that I'm not taking care of things properly – that you're not cared for adequately, that the house is depreciating in value because I didn't get it painted last year, that brother?... Besides, I thought I was getting the house."

Mother: "Well, I think it's important you both get an equal share. Equal is fair and it's important to me to be–"

Daughter: "Equal *effort* is fair. You've always sided with him. Ever since you decided I wasn't the perfect child – I wasn't going to be some beauty pageant queen, or ballerina, or whatever."

Mother: "My God, you're like an elephant. Can't you get over *anything?* You need to get some help, sorting this out, or you'll carry this with you forever. And it'll ruin your skin."

Daughter: "My skin? Are you for real? I don't know why I'm surprised. You should have just kept this quiet, instead of bringing up all this pain. Now I don't want to talk about it any more."

Mother: "Well, we need to talk about it now. We need to hammer out some kind of time table because it's going to take some doing for me to downsize enough to move into your back bedroom."

Daughter: "Whoa. This *is* a nightmare. You're planning to move in?"

Mother: "Well, that's what we've always talked about. I've been planning on it all along. You don't want me to spend my final years alone, do you? Have you suddenly upped and changed your mind?"

Daughter: "Mom, I have two teenage sons, with friends and girlfriends, and drum sets and, and lives. I work full-time. We talked about you moving in when Mike and I were still married. That was years ago. Without him, it's all up to me now and I don't know how long your health is going to hold out, and there's the car th–"

Mother: "I will *not* discuss the car again. This obsession you have over my driving. I've driven all my life and I will not let you think you can take that away. Dad said I should watch for this with you–"

Daughter: "Can you leave him out of this? Please. He's dead, for Christ's sake. Besides, he was nothing but trouble, and you should have–"

Mother: "I'm trying to stay on target here. This discussion is about my moving in. I am planning to move into your back bedroom and I want to know *when*. I want this to be a happy event. I want to work around your plans, of course, and do it in a convenient way–"

Daughter: "Mom, I can't handle much more. I just can't take on another –"

Mother: "– burden. So you think I'm a burden."

Daughter: "Those are your words, not mine. It's not about a burden. It's about taking care of you. I'm overwhelmed *now*. You'll want me to take you places and feel hurt when we do things as a family. I need space and well, you know, you like to control things. My house isn't like your's either – it's dirtier, less ordered -"

Mother: "So now I'm a control freak too? I don't need a list to tell me I'm not wanted. Maybe you should just admit it. Maybe your brother was right; you don't want to help me out. You're just so self centered that–"

Daughter: "Aha! So my brother *did* put you up to this! The two of you are in cahoots again. I wish–"

What's Said and Left Unsaid

This is a self-proving conversation. In it, it's easy to see the many ways we argue. We blame, manipulate, use guilt or shame, and seek revenge, etc., all in an attempt to get what we want: to prove we're okay, worthwhile, and right. Sometimes when we argue, we project the very things we hate most about ourselves onto the other person. Sometimes, the other person stings us with a comment that strikes at the very heart of whom we think we are. All the time, our identity feels threatened and we self prove.

The well-worn path of this particular conversation reflects many years of *not* addressing old hurts. As we've said before, these feelings don't go away. They stay with us and fester:

Feelings crave acknowledgment. Like free radicals, feelings wander around the conversation looking for some acknowledgment to hook onto. They won't be happy until they get it, and nothing else will do (Stone, Patton, and Heen, 2000, pp. 180).

In this dance of conflict, there are many examples of assumptions, mind-reading, and therapizing. Both Mother and Daughter finish one another's sentences and get distracted by numerous tangential conversations: over the brother, the dad, the Mother's needs and expectations, the car, cleanliness, finances; even the Daughter's skin. There is also a shadow conversation going on, about respect and independence.

As is often the case when intimates fight, there is a "secret struggle" as well – a mini-discussion flowing beneath even the shadow conversation. A secret struggle is all about feelings – they may be decades old but the feelings are still painfully raw. In this example, both Mother and Daughter are afraid the past mistakes and disappointments have wasted their relationship. Yet rather than broach this scary subject, they poke at it and each other with their sarcastic remarks. In short order, both will shut down and neither will hear or feel heard. In time, the tension will subside, but the hurt will remain; only to surface again, the next time they talk.

The Will – Take 2

This discussion offers many opportunities to change how Mother and Daughter deal with differences. Beginning with the tools discussed in Chapter One (denoted in italics and under-lined), the Mother could decide in advance, _which conversation_ she wants to have: to talk about the will, her moving in, or something else. She could tune into her Daughter's voice and body language, observe the moment the conversation begins to _shift_ and make a choice, whether or not to have the conversation now. Similarly, the Mother could _anticipate_ her Daughter's re-actions and come prepared with a variety of proposals. She could choose her words carefully and use _positive language_, trying to avoid inflammatory terms and accusations.

If the Mother decides to proceed with the conversation, either the Mother or Daughter could take a deep breath and Notice. They could concentrate their attention and Notice as a fly on the wall, taking in the entire situation. Either could elect to _interrupt the dance_; to remember that change begets change and try something altogether different. For example:

Mother: "I want to talk with you about the will."

Daughter: "Great idea! You've brought it up a
   bunch of times and I just haven't had the energy

to deal with it. Let's set a time and place and go
out to dinner and talk about it."

Alternatively, the Mother could try a different tact:

Mother: "I want to talk with you about the–"

Daughter: "The will. I know, I know. You've been
hinting about it for weeks. Mom, just let it go.
I know you're worried about the finances but
there's no reason to discuss it. I'm sure you
handled it just as you want. And we'll find out
about it when the time comes."

Mother: "What would be the best way for you and
me to have a conversation about the will?"

There are also ample opportunities for either person to
Notice and breathe, and _name their feelings_:

Daughter: "Equal *effort* is fair. You've always sided
with him. Ever since you decided I wasn't the
perfect child – I wasn't going to be some beauty
pageant queen, or ballerina, or whatever."

Mother: "My God, you're like an elephant. Can't
you get over *anything*? You need to get some
help with this, sorting it out, or you'll carry this
with you forever. And it'll ruin your skin."

Daughter: "Mom", breathing and Noticing, "This isn't
about my skin though, is it. I feel hurt by comments
like that. It's as though the only thing that's important to you is how I look. I feel sad and ashamed
about that kind of stuff – like I let you down. Plus,
we need to stay focused here; this is a life-changing
conversation. So, you were saying, about the will?"

Finally, this conversation is ripe for a _Beginner's Mind_ and to
Reflect *first*. Both Mother and Daughter are swamped by what

they assume they know. By adopting a Beginner's Mind, they could begin to let go of these assumptions and actually start to hear. They could Reflect *first*:

Mother: "Well, we need to talk about it now. We need to hammer out some kind of time table because it's going to take some doing for me to downsize enough to move into your back bedroom."

Daughter: "So, you're planning to move into the back bedroom at my house, is that right?"

Mother: "Well yes, of course. We've talked about this before. I need a place to live after all. You don't want me to end up in *a home*, do you?"

Daughter: "So, you're saying the reason you want to move into my back bedroom is because you don't want to move into a home, is that it?"

Mother: "Is this some kind of surprise to you? I have a very active life that I want to continue. I have Bridge and my work at the hospital. And I need a place to live that's convenient to all those things."

Daughter: "So you're saying that by moving into the back bedroom, you could continue your very active life."

Mother: "Yes, of course. The kids are there, they're almost driving age. And you'll be around. You know I like a lot of activity. I'll never be bored at your house."

Daughter: "So, with the kids driving, you're thinking they'll be able to take you to and from your appointments, work, and your activities, and when they aren't available, I will. And you'll enjoy all the commotion at the house. Right?"

Mother: "Well, yes. Well, um, I don't know. The kids do seem kind of busy, and you work all day long."

Reflect *first* invites the other person to say *more*. Normally, once the person speaking feels heard, the table turns for the other person to speak. The non-speaking person might say, "So, do you have anything else you want to say on this? Is it okay for me to talk now?" Alternatively, sometimes the person speaking runs out of things to say. He/she gets tired and decides nothing further needs to be said on this particular issue, and then the other person is free to speak. The person speaking might also "get clear" about what he/she really wants or means, and proceed to talk about that; or realize that what he/she wants isn't reasonable or possible, as in the above example. As she's speaking, the Mother realizes the kids are busy, her Daughter's away at work all day, and she may need to re-think her plans.

On occasion, when we Reflect *first*, we reflect wrong. This is actually a good thing because it gives the speaker a chance to immediately put the conversation back on track:

Mother: "Well yes, of course. We've talked about this before. I need a place to live after all. You don't want me to end up in *a home*, do you?"

Daughter: "So, you're saying the reason you want to move into my back bedroom is because you don't want to end up in a home, is that it?"

Mother: "I'm not saying that at all. I'm saying that ending up in a home is an option, and one I don't want. I want to move in with you because I want to be around the kids and spend more time with you."

By clarifying the Daughter's reflection, the Mother sheds more light on what's important to her.

The Will – Take 3

In keeping with our new definition of help, there are other techniques that don't involve "doing" for someone else. Again, the new definition accepts that both people are fully capable. Our task is not to tell another person what to do or what he/ she needs, it's to be present and work together to discover what's possible.

After the Daughter's comment about her brother, for example, the Mother could try _silence_. Too often we assume that silence needs to be filled. Yet prolonged silence is one way to be comfortable *not knowing*. It introduces spaciousness into the conversation. The Mother could Notice, adopt a Beginner's Mind, and sit quietly:

Daughter: "My brother. My brother. You're kidding, right? The brother who's two thousand miles away? The brother who's never been here to help with anything? The brother who sends little barbs over the phone, that I'm not taking care of things properly – that you're not cared for adequately, that the house is depreciating in value because I didn't get it painted last year, *that* brother?... Besides, I thought I was getting the house."

Mother: —

Daughter: "I love this house. I grew up in this house. I always assumed it would be mine. I just figured you knew that..."

The Mother could also inject _humor_. Humor is a "show-stopper." Like silence, it stops the conversation from taking a well-worn path; this time, by breaking the tension in the room. For example,

Mother: "Well, we need to talk about it now. We need to hammer out some kind of time table because it's going to take some doing for me to downsize enough to move into your back bedroom."

Daughter: "Whoa. This *is* a nightmare. You're planning to move in?"

Mother: "Well, *that* was a real ice breaker! Gotcha! Actually, I thought we had talked about this before...."

And then, being *transparent*, as described in Chapter One,

Mother: "Maybe what I should say is that I was *hoping* to move in with you. I was thinking I could be some help to you, with Mike gone and all. I just want to talk about it."

Finally, the Mother could try *reframing* the issue. Reframing re-castes the discussion in a broader context, ensuring it is not limited to a single frame or too narrow of a perspective:

Daughter: "Those are your words, not mine. It's not about a burden. It's about taking care of you. I'm overwhelmed *now.* You'll want me to take you places and feel hurt when we do things as a family. I need space and well, you know, you like to control things. My house isn't like your's either – it's dirtier, less ordered –"

Mother: "So, you're already feeling overwhelmed and I'm not even there! I'm wondering if this is really about how we each see the future unfolding. Perhaps we need to talk about how we see things – like spending time together, making sure we both feel safe and less stressed, having enough money to live comfortably, and things like that. Can we sit down and talk about that?"

Crystallized Reflection

Reflect *first* is not the same as "parroting". In fact, with care, we can use reflection as a way to crystallize what's being said. When we *Reflect first and crystallize*, we acknowledge our experience and invite the other person to help shape it by sharing their own. For example:

Mother: "I will *not* discuss the car again. This obsession you have over my driving. I've driven all my life and I will not let you think you can take that away. Dad said I should watch for this with you–"

Daughter: "This car thing is a hot button issue for both of us, isn't it? It sounds like you're saying, what's important is your current life style...your freedom and activities. Are you saying you want to keep your current lifestyle but not have the responsibility of owning a house? Is that it?"

Crystallized reflection is especially well-suited for dealing with the "secret struggle". Taking care not to step over the line and help by doing, we can take a deep breath and offer an idea...for discussion:

Mother: "So now I'm a control freak too? I don't need a list to tell me I'm not wanted. Maybe you should just admit it. Maybe your brother was right; you don't *want* to help me out. You're just so self centered that–"

Daughter: "You know Mom, I don't pretend to know how you feel or what the best way to resolve this is. I do feel we need to talk...and about a lot of things. When I listen to my snide remarks about Dad and all the anger I have towards my brother, and feel how nervous I am even talking with you about this stuff, it makes me sad. I really want to have a good relationship with you. You're my Mom and that's important to me. Do you think we could talk about *our relationship* at some point? About the hurts and the let-downs, and what we each wished had happened? And about how we *want* it to be? Could we do that together, at some point, in a safe way?"

A Different Kind of Knowing

Being present requires a greater level of awareness. It allows us to experience different ways of knowing; ways that are not related to doing, or winning, or needing to offer advice. When we are present, we connect with people: their body language, facial expressions, gestures, and their presence. We tune into the situation: the surroundings, the energy in the room, and the tension in the air; how we've positioned ourselves, if a table or desk is separating us, whether we can see the other person's face. We appreciate the vastness of what we *don't* know: what may have just happened, what other struggles they could be facing, what someone else may have said. When we are present, we accept that the **relationship is more important than the problem**, and we lead with that.

The fact is every conversation is a risk. No matter whom we're having it with; at the other end of the conversation is another person – someone who wants to be validated just as badly as we do. We're both taking a chance. To be present for another person, we sit right "on the razor's edge"; in the middle of the "very personal challenge of being affected, of being involved, of being engaged, of being available" (Sills, 2000, pp. 187). And there we make a choice: we can hurt or we can help – without doing.

AN AREA FOR FURTHER EXPLORATION

Being Present

Being *present* for another person in a conversation is a special skill. It's not something we cultivate naturally in today's world. In fact, it's quite the opposite of how most of us live. Being present requires a quiet mind and a sense of inner stillness. This is where Ayurveda can help.

According to Ayurveda, every experience affects us

---

mentally, emotionally, and physically. Using this knowledge, Ayurveda provides a personalized, daily routine to help us find and maintain a state of balance and inner calm. We already know there are five great elements that combine to create vital energies or body types: Vata (ether + air), Pitta (fire + water), and Kapha (water + earth). We also know that while we each have all three energies, we have them in a unique proportion.

The dominant elements comprising our body type dictate our basic constitution and tendencies: Vatas are airy and outgoing, Pittas are fiery and intense, and Kaphas are solid and steady. When our energies are in the proportion that Nature intended, we are said to be "in balance" and are at our best. When they are not, our more negative qualities emerge. Again, the goal is not to balance Vata, Pitta, and Kapha but to maintain our unique ratio of the three energies.

According to Ayurveda, every experience has the potential to throw us out-of-balance. To counter this, Ayurveda offers a daily routine tailored to our body type that covers all aspect of life. By following this regimen, we are able to quiet our mind and find a sense of inner stillness:

– Ayurveda suggests Vata people eat more warm food at regular times each day and eat sitting down. Also, go to bed and wake at regular times, say 10 pm and 6 am, and include some quiet, down-time each day. In terms of exercise and recreation, Ayurveda recommends *non-aerobic* activity such as swimming, horseback riding, walking and easy hiking, bowling, sailing, golf, canoeing, and nonviolent martial arts.

– For Pitta people, Ayurveda suggests reducing foods that are spicy, red, vinegar-based or acidic, too sour or salty. Also, eat more cooling foods, fruits, and stay away from alcohol. Pitta body types are encouraged to avoid too much sun and becoming overheated, especially at mid-day, and refrain from hard-driving, competitive activities, people, and situations. In terms of exercise and recreation, Ayurveda recommends *non-competitive* activities such as downhill skiing, mountain biking, touch football, ice skating, wind surfing, horseback riding, and swimming.

– For Kapha constitutions, Ayurveda suggests reducing dairy, wheat, sweet, oily, and heavy foods. Also, limit salt and try doing something active every day. Daily exercise, mental stimulation, getting outside, and trying new activities are especially important for Kaphas. Ayurveda recommends *aerobic* work-outs, cycling, calisthenics, racquetball, cross-country running, swimming, stair stepping, and lacrosse (See Anselmo & Brooks, 1996).

Ayurvedic principles apply to everything. Two Vatas in a relationship, for example, are apt to drive one another crazy, while a Vata and a Kapha have a balancing effect. A Pitta managing an office full of Pittas may become authoritarian, when, under other conditions, he/she may display a more collaborative management style. A Kapha on vacation in a dense, wet climate is likely to feel sick, lethargic, and depressed. As a general rule when it comes to people, places, and things: Vatas need to relax, Pittas need less heat, and Kaphas need more activity. These are the foundations of a steady, calm body/mind.

Chapter 8

Working with Others

If ever there was a place ripe for self proving, it would have to be work. The workplace is full of drama and intrigue; time-tables, deadlines, and the crisis of the moment. It's a place where personalities collide, assumptions abound, and identities reign supreme; of blame, shame, and possibly, fame...not to mention the day-to-day drudgery of churning out a product. Taken together, work is a breeding ground for self proving and conflict. The reasons for this are quite simple. First, there are a near limitless number of topics to fight about at work; from major issues to silly, petty things. If one considers the sheer volume of decisions made every day at a single firm – management, project execution, policies, technology, personnel, finance, hiring and firing, promotions – and multiplies that by the number of private, public, and non-for-profit organizations that exist – each is a conflict in the making.

Second, and more importantly, many of us get a huge chunk of our okay-ness from work. At work, we're someone special: the HR director, the project engineer, the foreman, the secretary to the assistant director for finance, the head of maintenance. We pride ourselves in how we do our work and how we're regarded by others. Work gives us a place and a position. It feeds *both* our primary fears, giving us a chance to feel good about ourselves and a place to belong. All of this adds up to many opportunities for conflict among many people, each competing for power, prestige, recognition, authority, control, and money.

Different and Yet...

In some respects, work is different than family; so work relationships and work-related conflict differ as well. Work has a defined mission, a hierarchy of control, and an organizational framework. It has operating procedures, written policies, prescribed competencies, performance standards, timelines, and assignments. Work has detailed tasks to be completed, a product to deliver, and a financial sheet to balance. It is regulated and controlled, legislated and administered, quantified and measured, contracted and ordered...and led, directed, and supervised.

The workplace is also divided into groups – departments, sections, units, and divisions. Much of what gets done at work is accomplished through groups, and most groups depend on one another for various aspects of the final product. Group membership is a powerful motivator. It creates a feeling of loyalty and cohesion, a sense of common ownership and connection. Groups can accomplish what no single individual can. They enable managers to blend unique skill sets, stimulate productivity, and foster creativity. When group members have a well-articulated objective, share a common purpose and commitment, are self-motivated and imaginatively managed, the potential of a group is unlimited.

Groups also bring with them a fair amount of problems. By including some, groups exclude others: individuals who identify with and are "positively attached" to a group often "assign negative stereotypes" to non-members, "viewing them with suspicion and hostility" (Tomlinson and Lewicki, 2006, pp. 220 [citing Tajfel and Turner, 1985]). As a consequence, groups are highly prone to black/white thinking, framing issues in terms of insiders and outsiders, either/or, and this or nothing. They are also disposed to "group think", a condition in which all members start to think the same. This kind of contracted thinking paralyzes innovation and can mire a company in a "this is the way it's always been done" mentality. Additionally, concerns over reputation, saving face, relative importance, and belonging take on greater significance in groups; members can even act against their better judgment for fear of being cast out of the group.

Conflict in the workplace is full of strategies and tactics which often revolve around positional bargaining. Groups make demands of one another, threaten and cajole, play games, invoke authority, engage in tit-for-tat, fractionalize problems, and create larger, umbrella issues as a way to stall progress (See Folger, Poole, and Stutman, 2005, pp. 255-267). They may enlist the help of outside sources such as boards, legislators, or the media. In meetings, both sides may attempt to control the agenda, manipulatively shift topics, attack one another's legitimacy or expertise, threaten to leave if their demands are not met, or "narrowcaste" their position, presenting only the most "supportive information...while avoiding those [sources] that are critical" (Burgess and Burgess, 2006, pp. 182). In other words, they self prove.

Individuals battle at work too, often relying on the same self proving tactics. They stir the pot, create new problems, rally their peers, and ostracize outsiders. They misrepresent the facts, mislead their superiors, gossip and slander a colleague, and circuitously push their own agenda. The source of conflict runs the gamut, from office politics to office romance; from product safety to a perceived slight. As authors Stone, Patton, and Heen point out, one would be astounded just "how often difficult conversations are wrapped up in both people reacting to what the conversation seems to be saying about them" (2000, pp. 127).

Through all of this, one thing is certain: work-related conflict is incredibly draining. Whether the discord is between individual employees, within a group, among departments, or across companies, work-related conflict wastes time and money at all levels of the organization. All too often, we learn one fact too late in our careers: *relationships last.* Before, during, and after a disagreement, people are still expected to work together. Yesterday's adversary can be tomorrow's supervisor; future projects, reorganizations, and mergers can bring previously warring factions into the same department or product delivery schedule; and opposing parties in different organizations often share the same friends, colleagues, and future bosses. One may even end up looking for a job one day, with "the enemy".

Just Like Family

Despite these differences, conflict happens at work for the same reasons it happens in our intimate relationships: when our identity feels threatened, we re-act out of habit. Groups are, after all, made up of individuals and every individual brings his/her "self" to work: our strengths and weaknesses, personal values, bedrock principles, and deepest fears. We come with our stuck perceptions and feelings, fixed assumptions, and behavior that needs to change. We fall back on the same re-active mind ruts to protect and defend ourselves that we use at home, and are just as likely – if not more so – to choose a side, try to control things, and shut out new ideas. And because our self worth is so tied up in the mission at work and our personal success, we're at even greater risk: our identity is intimately linked to what happens at the office and feels very much at stake when things don't go our way.

Framing is also commonplace at work, and group frames can be especially powerful:

A new CEO decides to consolidate independent project offices across program areas to save money and streamline oversight. Unfortunately, she's only been in the job for a month and has already met with a mixed reaction. She decides to empanel a committee of affected managers to consider the pros and cons of the consolidation plan. At their first meeting, the managers decide the idea is ridiculous, and, with that frame in mind, proceed to write a report confirming their position. The CEO has her own ideas and is insulted by the report. A contest of wills ensues, and ultimately, the party with the most power, wins. But not before reputations are sullied and future relationships, promotions, and possible good ideas are jeopardized.

As in any setting, feelings lie at the heart of conflict at work and rarely, if ever, do they get the attention they deserve. Even the most mundane arguments involve feelings: a colleague may be angry if she thinks her competence is being questioned; annoyed by the power grab of a former friend and associate; irate over a bonus she felt she deserved; irritated with staff who aren't pulling their weight; or resentful for being passed over for a promotion. Given the professional bias at work, we are especially prone to want to frame a problem "exclusively as a substantive disagreement", hoping we can avoid having to confront the hurt feelings it embodies (Stone, Patton and Heen, 2000, pp. 87). Yet as we all know, feelings can't be shoved under the rug at work or anyplace else. They re-surface again, in time.

Just as at home, we rush to solutions at work. In fact, the tendency to "hurry up and fix things" is especially strong at work because appearances are so important. When we rush to solutions, we never get beyond positions. We never get to the interests, needs, feelings, and intentions that drive our positions and broaden the possibilities. At home, when a husband announces he's decided to sell the antique hutch and replace it with a new television, it sparks an argument; when all he really wanted was to watch NASCAR on a wide screen TV. Similarly, when a manager gets in the middle of a problem and "decides" how to solve it, the real concerns never get raised, nor do the misperceptions get cleared up. The situation may appear resolved, but not for long.

What We Bring to Work

Just as in any other setting, our Mental Locks underlie conflict in the workplace: we assume everyone sees the world as we do, or at least they should; and that we know what other people are saying, how they feel, and what they need. When we add in money, ambition, prestige, and power to the equation, work can be a pretty toxic place.

People don't just bring their hopes and dreams to work; they bring their imbalances as well. More often than not, work makes them worse. Many people, for example, lead very stressful lives. We already know that too much stress can damage organs, make us more susceptible to disease, and cause us to have a "lower threshold" for emotions like anger. When our experience at work *adds* to this pressure, our ability to function is seriously undermined. As Maxwell Gladwell found in his book <u>Blink</u>:

> Most of us, under pressure, get too aroused, and past a certain point, our bodies begin shutting down so many sources of information that we start to become useless (2005, pp. 225).

This means our perspective contracts, our judgment narrows, and our creativity fades away; just the opposite of what we need to do a good job.

This situation is aggravated by the recent proliferation of gadgetry at work. Gadgets require our constant attention. E-mail, for example, creates the additional stress of "so many e-mails to answer". Similarly, cell phones spawn the need to stay continuously in touch with the office and others, even on vacation. For the individual, the net result can be an inability to sit still; a temporary "Attention Deficit Disorder" where we text-message and return e-mails during meetings, or excuse ourselves to take "this important call". We become addicted to activity, unable to sit alone or endure a silent moment.

When a stressed-out person works in a stressful place, the collision affects everyone. Keeping with our Ayurvedic schematic, Vatas re-act to stress by taking on more to do. They work at a frenzied pace, becoming increasingly fretful and anxious which spreads throughout the office. A hot-headed Pitta person will likely take control: he/she may begin shouting orders, skip lunch to get more done, and try to figure out who's to blame. Kaphas re-act to stress by shutting down. They feel ill and might rationalize going home sick. In other words, Vatas pursue, Pittas decide to fix the problem, and Kaphas avoid it.

When conflict erupts at work, each body type causes its own set of secondary problems. Vatas work very fast, but not necessarily smart. They may give up quickly, recommend a totally new but untested approach, or do something impulsive. Pittas "assume they know" more than the other two types. They ignite conflict, cause hurt or hard feelings, or raise the overall temperature with their authoritative manner. Kaphas dig in their heels. They avoid change and conflict at all costs. These re-actions support research which shows that work-related conflict is related to increased absenteeism, decreased productivity, a greater potential for injury on the job, and reduced objectivity (See www. occupationalhazards.com/articles/12168).

Moreover, according to Ayurveda, we tend to indulge in *more* of what we need the *least*, which is the origin of disease. After a stressful day at the office, a Vata person is apt to grab a quick salad and spend his/her leisure time taking a fast-paced, aerobic dance class. A Pitta person may have a spicy dinner and go play a competitive game of tennis. And a Kapha person may overeat and take a nap. We show up for work the next day in even worse shape. Thus, not only do we bring our imbalances to work where they grow more pronounced, the cycle perpetuates itself until the pattern is finally interrupted.

Climbing Out

Fortunately, we are not destined to battle at work. As we've seen, work-related conflict happens for the same reasons it does in any other setting, and we already know the first two keys for changing how we deal with differences: the power of Compassion – of Noticing, taking a deep breath, and trying something different, and the power of Forgiveness and Reflect *first*. We simply need to apply what we've learned to the workplace.

The biggest impediment is taking that first step: the hardest part of dealing with differences is often sitting down, face-to-face, with someone with whom we strenuously disagree. To do this, we have to remember that what's going on is identity-based and involves a lot of self proving; we *both* feel threatened and are trying to protect ourselves. We have to recall that behavior is a choice, and we can personally attest to just how hard it is to interrupt a habit of choice. We also need to remember that regardless of what the other person is saying or doing, it makes sense to him or her; it's functional, even if we don't understand it. Finally, we need to be aware how connected we are, especially at work. Interdependence is the nature of work: every person depends on every other person to get the job done. That's why relationships last.

Making it Work

Conflict at work is a chance to practice what we've learned. Consider the following scenario:

A CEO of a major technology company – who's trained to know the answers and accustomed to being in charge – is approached about a new medical billing system by a Board Member known for being difficult to deal with. Almost immediately, the CEO feels intimidated and hunkers down into her re-active combat mode: he's saying, "What do you think about this?" and she's hearing, "Why aren't you on top of this?" He's saying, "How do you think you'll be handling this?" and she's hearing,

"If you were competent, you'd know what's going on!"

As the conversation progresses, she begins to feel warm and anxious. She makes several attempts to end the conversation and save face, but the Board Member persists. The more he talks, the more she assumes: "This guy never really liked me"; "He's a jerk. He's always been out to get me"; "He doesn't know what he's talking about. I've reviewed more billing systems than he's ever heard about"; "I know he's trying to one-up me. He needs to put me down to look good."

Soon, she starts to worry – about her reputation, her authority, her career. Finally, feeling cornered, she draws a line in the sand: she raises her voice, digs in her heels on an issue she knows nothing about, and delivers an ultimatum. And to send the message home, she repeats her position even louder as though the Board Member is deaf...which he is, to her reality!

Now, let's consider the same conversation given what we've learned so far, with the CEO accepting from the onset, that neither party shares the same reality. With this awareness, the discussion becomes an exchange, a dialogue and not a danger:

Board Member: "What do you think about this new medical billing system?"

CEO: "Which new medical billing system?"

Board Member: "Don't you read industry magazines? Why aren't you on top of this stuff? It's your job *to know*, you know. You've got to see how important this is..."

The CEO feels the tension rise. Instead of re-acting and trying to defend herself or challenge him as she would normally, she decides to Notice. Noticing gives her a chance to breathe. She elects to be silent to allow the Board Member to say more:

> Board Member: "What, you're not responding today? I know you want to be a team player. But we need a vision! This company can't survive without *someone* at the top having at least some kind of vision. Don't you know this is your job?"

The CEO recognizes the Board Member is self proving. She understands that he assumes he knows what she's feeling and needs to do, and believes "to help" means inserting himself and asserting his ideas. She decides to adopt a Beginner's Mind and be comfortable *not knowing*. With this awareness, she is able to Reflect *first*:

> CEO: "You're right. It *is* a key part of my job and I've got a pretty full plate right now. Why don't you tell me something about the particular system you're interested in?"
>
> Board Member: "Frankly, I'm still concerned. I know you don't think this kind of stuff is important. But it doesn't look good that *I'm* on top of this and you're not."

The Board Member seems to be waiting for an answer. He's staring her down. So the CEO tries something different,

> CEO: "And?"
>
> Board Member: "Well, the system is put out by Medical Matters and is reportedly up for sale. I'm told it has everything doctors, small medical groups, all the way up to what major hospitals need to meet the new federal guidelines and reduce insurance reimbursement time by half."

The CEO knows that together, they have the resources to handle this matter on their own. She decides to Reflect *first* in a way that crystallizes what the Board Member has just said:

CEO: "You sound really excited about this – a new system, put out by a solid company that you know well, with a potential market that's huge. It sounds like this is a major buy-out opportunity for us. What are your thoughts?"

Board Member: "Isn't that *your* job? Do you want me to make the phone call for you too?"

The CEO Notices again and takes another deep breath. She decides to name the feeling she's experiencing and be transparent:

CEO: "Look, I'm feeling kind of nervous and irritated here. We seem to be dancing around something. I can't possibly be on top of everything, and I'm comfortable with the time I put in here and my commitment to the company. If you would like to talk about how I'm handling my job, then perhaps we should do that at a time that's good for both of us. My contract's up for renewal soon and I would like to talk about what you think makes a good CEO. In the meantime, I'd like to get on top of this billing system and a little bit more information would be really helpful."

At this point, the conversation could go in several directions. The Board Member could pick up on the CEO's transparency and set a date to discuss her job performance. Alternatively, he could decide that her job is not the issue and shift the conversation back to the billing system. Whatever happens, she wants to continue to Reflect *first*, to draw him out because both issues are important:

Board Member: "I'm not questioning your commitment. Really. I'm just surprised, that's all. If we were to purchase this system, it would be a boon for our medical department. And, it's fallen behind every other part of the company."

The CEO begins to *hear*. She creates enough space for the Board Member to speak, and continues to Reflect *first* until he's convinced she understands:

CEO: "You've mentioned the medical department before. You're really concerned about that, aren't you?"

Board Member: "Well, I used to work there. Did you know that? When I left, it was the top performing department in the company."

CEO: "That's got to be incredibly frustrating. All that hard work...and to see it go to waste..."

Board Member: "I'd like to leave with it on top again. I'd like that to be my legacy. I've only got a couple years left on the board, you know."

CEO: "So, you'd like me to work with you on making that medical department strong again, is that right?"

Board Member: "That's absolutely right! I think there's a lot of potential there. It's just under-utilized."

CEO: "I just want to make sure there's not something else here we need to talk about. I am more than willing to sit down and talk about what kind of a CEO you feel this company needs."

Board Member: "Well, I would like to talk with you about my vision for the company. I just feel like we can do so much more."

CEO: "So, how would you like to proceed from here?"

In this example, the CEO doesn't back down, nor did she fail to communicate her own concerns. By understanding what's happening and why – how both people feel threatened, have locked down mentally, and need to self prove – she's able to put the techniques to work. She avoids an unnecessary confrontation and the repercussions of digging in her heels. Most importantly, she preserves the relationship.

Being Present at Work

Work-related conflict is by no means limited to the corporate world. Government is notorious for intergovernmental struggles, discord between agencies, and disagreements within and among policy makers. Similarly, conflict abounds in the non-profit sector, on community boards, as well as in small private and family-owned firms. Even the spiritual community has its quarrels. There is, for example, a long-standing debate in the Yoga community over the "physical-ness" of yoga. Many Yoga teachers push a progressively more difficult yoga practice. Others suggest that over time, yoga should become less physical, focusing instead on attaining the "higher states of Yoga" (Stryker, 2007, pp. 19). Nor is the mediation field immune to conflict; where recurring arguments include how directive a mediator should be, what neutrality means, and whether an agreement among parties is the goal of mediation.

What's important to remember is that with the right understanding of what motivates conflict and why we act the way we do, the techniques and tools flow naturally and can be adapted to any setting. With that understanding, it becomes easier and more desirable to slow the pace and be present with whatever's happening; no matter how threatened we feel. We don't need the conversation to validate who we think we are or who we want to be; and we don't assume we know who the other person is or needs to be, either.

Choosing the Relationship

In the book <u>Crucial Confrontations</u>, the authors suggest that management means more than being in charge; that being the boss means *making the job doable.*

The best leaders don't simply inspire people...they help make [the task] easy...They are facilitators, enables, and supporters, not armed guards or cheerleaders" (Patterson, Grenny, McMillan, and Switzler, 2005, pp. 151).

Similarly, in his book Good to Great, author Jim Collins discusses what he calls "Level 5 Leadership", including that we "look out the window to attribute success to factors other than [ourselves]...and in the mirror [when things go poorly]" (2001, pp. 38). We could add to this, another suggestion: part of a manager's job is to *preserve relationships*...in fact, it's part of everyone's job.

Preserving relationships at work begins by recognizing that work is a relationship among equals; separated by age and time, education and experience, and perhaps, a simple twist of fate. It means as managers, we can't be afraid to apologize when we're wrong; or ask the ultimate question: "If you ran this place, what would you do to solve this problem?" (Patterson, Grenny, McMillan, and Switzler, 2005, pp. 165). Most importantly, to preserve relationships, we need to lead by example: in the face of conflict at work, we need to ask the questions that allow us to practice what we've learned. For example:

–   When conflict appears to be escalating quickly, we might ask: *"Is this approach working for you?"* or *"Do you think this is getting us closer to or farther away from where we want to be?"*

–   When someone is about to leave to room in anger, we might say, *"What would make it okay for you to stay and discuss this?"*

–   When the situation appears to be at a standstill, we might ask: *"How would you like to proceed?"*, *"What would you like to do next?"*, or *"What do you think the next steps are?"* and,

–   When the same issues keep re-surfacing, we might say, *"Do you think any amount of conversa-*

tion will resolve this? If not, are we free to move on?"

We might also try to make better use of the word "and", as demonstrated in the above example, using it as an opener to allow the other person to say more. We can stick with "I statements". "I statements" lead with "I" instead of "You", and focus on how *we* feel or what we need instead of what we think the other person feels or needs. Finally, when totally stuck, we might try switching places and arguing the other person's point of view.

In the final analysis, the ultimate measure of a manager is the satisfaction of his/her employees and the ultimate measure of an employee is the satisfaction of his/her customers. This calls for a new kind of daily performance measure we apply to ourselves. We stop, Notice, breathe, and Reflect internally:

- Am I talking more than listening?
- How many times have I said the word "I"?
- How long can I endure silence? Can I *not* take this call?
- What other explanations are there for this person's behavior?
- Do I know my intentions? Why am I doing this?
- Am I able to allow others to solve their problem, in their way?

It all comes back to Compassion and Forgiveness. At work, Forgiveness takes a special form. We acknowledge:

We ourselves are not above such things, that in another time and another place we might have done the same, that all of us are flawed and often act less than our best – only then can we...forgive (Richmond, 2000, pp. 161).

And yet, even with all of this, it's not quite enough to fully change how we deal with differences.

AN AREA FOR FURTHER EXPLORATION

Being Present

"How can I do this?" you might ask, "How can I, in the middle of an argument, make a deliberate and conscious choice to use Compassion and Forgiveness while some guy is screaming at me? It's counter-intuitive!" Actually, there's a trick that can help: it's called the *preya and shreya*. Preya and Shreya are tools for looking at a situation. Being able to distinguish between the two gives us the guidance we need to make a deliberate choice.

According to the Yogic tradition, every choice involves a preya and a shreya (See Easwaran 1992:30-41). The preya refers to what's pleasurable, what gives us immediate, and usually sense-related, pleasure. There's nothing wrong with sense-related pleasure. The problem is when we crave it, desperately. Then, pleasure-seeking behavior becomes a mind rut that rules over us. This applies to every situation: the problem isn't wanting, or wanting more; it's wanting more *for me* that's destructive. Shreya, on the other hand, is a more mature form of pleasure: its pleasure over the longer term. It's what's good or beneficial over the long haul:

> Preya is that which pleases us, which tickles the ego. Shreya..[is neither] pleasing or displeasing. It simply means what benefits us...improves our health...or peace of mind (ibid., 31).

In a conflict or any emotionally charged situation, we can anticipate the preya and shreya. The preya will always be what would feel good right now: saying that snide remark, giving that perfect piece of advice, rattling off the litany of past hurts, or screaming, "I quite!"

The preya is a re-action, a habitual way of thinking or behaving. The shreya is influenced by our inner wisdom. It asks us to override habit, interrupt the pattern, and make a more enlightened choice. To find the shreya requires Noticing, taking a breath, and listening.

So, in response to a nasty letter that hurt our feelings and threatened our sense of self, we may well write back an equally nasty reply. Then we Notice, breathe, listen, and ask: Does it take more courage to send this or not to send it? It's our choice...

Changing the World

Chapter 9

When Doing the
Right Thing Isn't

We've been talking about a different way of dealing with differences – in our relationships, at home, and in the workplace – when our *personal* identity feels threatened. We have a *social* identity as well. Our social identity reflects the groups we identify with. While we're each involved in many groups, some are more important than others and those are the ones that shape our social identity. Conflict is most intractable when our personal and social identity team up and *both* are threatened. Typically, we tackle these crises with one thing in mind: to solve the problem our way.

A Social Identity

Our social identity involves our primary affiliations; the ethnic, religious, cultural, political, philosophical, and cause-based groups we identify with. It may be tied to a community issue or one that transports us to the world stage: we can be committed to promoting locally-grown produce, unionized labor, a cure for breast cancer, or a two-state solution to the Palestinian/Israeli situation. Most of what's been written about social (also called "collective") identity conflict pertains to large-scale conflict of an ethno-political nature, which is extremely complex and intractable. Social identity conflict happens in smaller groups as well. It can arise over any issue, mission, or problem we feel passionate about; one that's worth fighting for.

Our social identity is generally an extension of our personal identity. We belong to groups that share and confirm our views. Like work, our group affiliations feed both our primary fears: they give us a chance to feel good about ourselves and a place to belong. In our groups, we're among people who have a common sense of purpose, share our beliefs, and hold similar values. As author Christopher Moore tells us:

> Values are freely chosen internal standards that people use to judge whether issues, behaviors, or events are good-bad, right-wrong, moral-immoral...The development of values is the result of a complex socialization process...the end result [of which] is an elaborate set of beliefs [that] rarely change dramatically during the life of an individual or group (Moore, 2003, pp. 401).

Moore distinguishes between three types of values: moral, terminal, and operational. Moral values represent our deepest beliefs and govern such issues as gender, honesty, and equality. Terminal values relate to many areas of our lives such as lifestyle, politics, and religion. Operational values reflect our preferences and attitudes (ibid., pp. 402-3).

Our social identity is mainly associated with our moral and terminal values. We may belong to a group that believes there's only one way to God and it's through our church; or sees affirmative action as essential; or believes nature is a collective responsibility. We may belong to a group that sees school prayer as the American way, or regards it as an invasion of privacy; that's committed to free-trade with China, or condemns it as sending high-salary manufacturing jobs overseas; that believes dog racing is cruel, or sees it as a Friday night's entertainment. The point is we tend to belong to groups that share our personal beliefs, and provide us with an opportunity to affirm, exercise, and extend those beliefs. When that opportunity is frustrated or undermined in some way, conflict is the result.

The Third Mental Lock

Social identity conflict is "arguably the most destructive force on the planet" (Burgess and Burgess, 2006, pp. 183). It is complicated, highly emotional, and intractable, in large part because it involves our moral and terminal values which change very slowly, if at all. It arises over issues of the deepest concern; often involving matters of religion, culture, politics, and our world view.

Social identity conflict is "rooted in" our "collective need for dignity, recognition, safety, control, purpose, and efficacy" (Rothman, 1997, pp. 7). The situations in Darphor, Rwanda, and the Middle East are perhaps the best examples of social identity conflict, where entire peoples believe their dignity, their "existential needs and values" (ibid., pp. 9), their very survival is at stake. The national debate over abortion, gay marriage, and immigration are also examples of social identity conflict; as are "many labor-management conflicts" where "control [and] participation" issues are at stake (ibid.), and quality of life concerns such as where repeat sex offenders are allowed to live, the citing of coal-burning plants, and the closing of local churches.

Social identity conflict threatens *both* our social and personal identity. It undermines how we see ourselves as individuals and as members of a group, and attacks what we value most. In such situations, our sense of self feels at risk; along with every other person's sense of self in our group. Everyone's ego is in overdrive, everyone's mind is on automatic pilot, and everyone's identity is on the line. With so much at stake, we shut down mentally. We reject any idea that differs from our own; we contract. We can only hear our collective stories, recall our past hurts, and see one way out. We engage the third Mental

Lock: **we assume there's one right way.** This Lock applies to individual conflict, at home and at work, and to social identity conflict. In the latter case, often every member of the group locks onto this belief: we believe there's only one right way and it's our way. We're "doing the right thing" – there's only one and we know what it is.

How We Prove "There's One Right Way"

In social identity conflict, when we engage the third Mental Lock, we take part in a kind of "institutionalized self proving." In its more benign forms, institutionalized self proving often involves the following, we:

(1) <u>Use Inflammatory Language</u>. The issue is already severely polarized; we then use language to sharpen the divide. We paint our perspective as the only right and reasonable choice, while the other party's view is wrong. The language of social identity conflict is dramatic, self righteous, and antagonistic: we're not sad, we're horrified; we're not supportive, we're patriotic; they're not people, they're terrorists. Such language fires up the group and flames the controversy. It reflects a long but selective memory of past events, and a short-term horizon of what needs to be done. Consider the following:
   - "They can either get at the truth or make it a political spectacle";
   - "We can either give a woman a window into her womb and help her make the right decision, or pretend she can do it on her own";
   - "We can either attack militarily and care, or don't and ignore the problem";
   - "You are either with the troops and ready to ensure they're prepared for battle, or against America."

Using language to prove there's one right way is supported by many interests, including the media, talk show hosts, religious leaders, and lobbyists. According to National Public Radio, for example, an estimated 13.5 million Americans tune into the Rush Limbaugh Show alone, every day (All Things Considered, 1/25/07). When we grow so invested in one right way, it becomes impossible to admit mistakes. We can never sit down with those who oppose us...out of fear.

(2) <u>Attribute the Worst</u>. Especially in social identity conflict, we attribute the worst motives to anyone who disagrees with us while we're far "more charitable" with members of our own group (Stone, Patton, and Heen, 1999, pp. 46-7). In other words, we assume we know *and* assume the worst. Moreover, we often mis-take "bad intentions" as proof the people *themselves* are bad (ibid., pp. 48-9). As a result, not only are we justified in opposing them, but we can dismiss them out-of-hand. Once we adopt this frame of mind, it becomes a self-fulfilling prophecy: "we begin to see what we feel" and grow "blind to the needs and suffering of the other side" (Maiese, 2006, pp. 188). We can, for example, blindly assume that all ATV enthusiasts don't respect the environment; Israel is justified in using excessive force against Hezboulah; and the United States should abide by a foreign policy of not talking with its enemies. By attributing the worst to anyone who disagrees with us, we never risk hearing another view.

(3) <u>Invoke a Moral Imperative</u>. Whenever one group believes it's doing the right thing, everyone

else is, by definition, wrong. We invoke a moral imperative and attribute a sense of right-ness to everything we say and do. We declare the church, the country, even God, is behind us. Backed by such an imperative, we're far more likely to see those who agree with us "as motivated by ethics and principle" and those who don't as driven by "narrow self-interest" (Vedantum, Albany Times Union, 3/18/07). Moreover, once we assume we are inherently right, we're free to blame others for anything that goes wrong. We "view the source of conflict as external" (Rothman, 1997, pp. 27) while the answer rests with us. We never need to consider an alternative solution.

When Hate is Part of Conflict

When we assume there's one right way, *we become attached to specifics.* We fight over how we see the problem, what the goal is, and how to get there. Not surprisingly, in such situations, many groups resort to positional bargaining; with two immutable positions, positional tactics tend to harden views and separate the sides even further. Unfortunately, interests-based negotiations don't generally work in these situations either. Issues such as survival, dignity, safety, control, and recognition are not easily converted into interests; nor are they amenable to compromise, at least not initially (ibid., pp. 9). As a consequence, social identity conflict often spans decades, lifetimes, and even generations. In time, it warps into hate.

According to author Rush Dozier, hate is an extreme form of fear. In his book, <u>Why We Hate</u>, Dozier suggests that hate is the combination of the human survival instinct + meaning (See Dozier, 2002). He argues that due to the connection between the limbic area of the brain (which houses our emotions, primal fears, desires, likes, and dislikes) and the more evolved neo-cortex, we are able to "interpret differences in meaning as threats to our survival" (ibid., pp. 10, 12). Thus, when a group disagrees with something that has meaning to us, we can learn to hate them. The limbic system, which is the more primitive area of the brain and acts in a pre-conscious manner, "pre-empts" the more advanced neural system and instead of reflective thought, we re-act (ibid., pp. 18, 233). Dozier warns,

> History makes it painfully apparent that when hate pervades a meaning system, there is virtually no limit to the atrocities an individual, group, or society can perpetrate (ibid., pp. 13).

Dozier distinguishes between anger and hate. Anger, he suggests, can be selective and transient. Hate, on the other hand, reflects the characteristics of the primitive mind: we generalize, think in terms of black and white, grow self-possessed, and obsess about the past which we remember in a selective and highly personalized manner (ibid., pp. 228-233). Stereotypes are part of hate. Dozier suggests stereotypes are first formed in the primitive brain, become prejudice through our meaning systems, and are then rationalized in the more advanced brain (ibid., pp. 41). When we stereotype, we generalize from our experiences or perceived experiences and paint entire groups with a broad-brush; we make them less than fully human. We then "nurture these meanings and the memories that ensconce them and support our bias" (LeBaron, 2002, p. 106), and transmit these calcified views to our children and our children's children.

When our group believes it's doing the right thing and we infuse that belief with enough meaning, fear, aggression, and hate, it can easily justify the more extreme forms of institutionalized self proving: pre-emptive strikes in the absence of an imminent threat, religious persecution, domination, occupation, war, and genocide. We learn to hate what we don't understand and rationalize it every step of the way. Dozier tells us, it takes a "competition of ideas" to "have a profound effect" (2002, pp. 14).

In Search of Something Solid

At its deepest level, every form of conflict, social and personal alike, is a search for something solid. We're looking for something stable and secure; something to hold on to. This is a uniquely human search. It's also a form of resistance. Resistance occurs whenever we try to avoid what is; which is not to say we should submit when we believe something is unfair or unjust, or forfeit our point of view. We should always stand up for what we think is right and there are many causes, both social and personal, worth fighting for. But hearing an alternative point of view is not the same as agreeing with it; it's not the same as resignation. In fact, when we refuse to hear another point of view because it differs from our own, we're being afraid. It's that simple.

Searching for something solid is pretty typical human behavior; it's one of the ways we self prove. Yet it runs contrary to some universal truths. The Buddhist tradition, for example, tells us everything is always *changing;* nothing stands still, not even for an instant. Change happens on a molecular level, in our thoughts, inside our bodies, in the conditions around us, in others, and in the world at large. We are not the same person we were yesterday because yesterday changed us. Every field of knowledge is in a constant state of flux as ideas are fleshed out, disproved, and new concepts take their place. Nothing stays the same. As a result, nothing lasts. In Buddhism, this it called the second stain of existence: everything in life is *impermanent.* This means that nothing is ever final:

> Impermanence is painful because we want the good things to last. We long for stability and safety...We orient ourselves in relation to fixed reference points – durable

objects, regular patterns, repetition, habits, laws, and eternal truths...We identify with them and derive our identity from them (Leifer, pp. 81, 84-5).

Finally, there is nothing to hold on to, known in Buddhism as *groundlessness*. Try as we may, there's no leg to stand on, no philosophy or belief that will protect us, no rug that can't be pulled out from under us.

Every person alive faces the challenges of change, impermanence, and groundlessness. As we've seen, most of us re-act by holding on even tighter: we fall back on patterned behaviors, worn-out perceptions, stereotypes, and hate to help us feel safe. We assume we're right, that there's one right way...our way.

A National Mind Rut

In his book Power, Faith, and Fantasy, author Michael Oren chronicles America's relationship with the Middle East from the beginning of this country to the present-day. He traces how early missionaries, "deeply imbued with the American ideals of individualism, civic virtue, and patriotism", went to the Middle East "'determined to lift mankind to a higher and better plane of living'" and bring their best "'to the heathen world'" (2007, pp.82 [quoting Oliver Elsbree]). Early on, he writes, "The Americans invariably assumed...cruelty...was endemic to Islam", and believed wholeheartedly in the primacy of their form of governance, "regarding the region's autocratic rulers with a blend of abhorrence and contempt" (ibid., pp. 154). By the 1930's, Americans spoke of a Middle East that "was the victim of 'Moslem fanaticism, with its fatalistic belief that what happens is the 'Will of Allah'" (ibid., pp. 439). Some views change very little with time.

The beliefs that feed social identity conflict are mental ruts. They are deeply ingrained and sometimes, centuries old. Once imbedded, these habits are nearly impossible to break.

As the above depicts, language fuels us, we attribute the worst motives to those we don't understand, and we back-up our actions with a moral imperative. Our stereotypes die especially hard, as we pass them on generation to generation.

Speaking about American foreign policy in general, the authors of <u>Ethical Realism</u> highlight the mistake we make when we try to "divide the world into clear areas of black and white, good and evil":

> [This] has led above all to the determined refusal to study or understand the power of local nationalism, whether reflected in Communism, Islamism, or other phenomena ((Lieven and Hulsman, 2006, 40-1).

In other words, when we assume there is one right way, we never consider alternatives. We never investigate or study how and why we differ. We never see beyond our narrow and contracted views, and imagine the possibilities. Worse still, we overlook the most obvious point: that we *each* have one right way – one right way of seeing the problem, one right way of resolving the situation, and one right set of outcomes. There are *two*. There are, in fact, far more than two.

AN AREA FOR FURTHER EXPLORATION

The Interconnected Mind

In addition to body types, Ayurveda offers an understanding of our mental capacities as well. In <u>Ayurveda and the Mind</u>, author David Frawley explains that the mind is an instrument for "deriving information from the external world"; the brain is the organ through which the mind operates; and the mind is the vehicle through which awareness works (1996, pp. 48-49). He argues that since the mind can be observed, we are not the mind. He describes the mind as pervading the entire body and able to "motivate [the body] as a whole"; dualistic, "like all matter...[and] prone to ambivalence or extremes"; and comprised of "nothing but thought" (ibid., pp. 54-55).

Ayurveda divides the mind into five levels: the Higher Self, Inner Consciousness, Intelligence, Sense Mind, and the Ego; again, reflecting the five elements of either, air, fire, water, and earth, respectively. The Sense Mind and Ego are the aspects of which we are most familiar. Both are comprised of Conditioned Consciousness, pure energy contracted down and conditioned by repetitive thoughts, actions, and feelings.

In Ayurveda, individual intelligence – or "book learning" – is considered a lower form of Intelligence (ibid., pp. 96). Intelligence gives us the capacity to understand, discern, and make choices. The Inner Consciousness and Higher Self harbor our inner wisdom; it is the kind of awareness we seek to enhance through our daily experiences, including how we deal with differences and be present in our relationships.

According to Ayurveda, *the heart* is the center of Consciousness: whereas the head is the center of the Sense Mind, the heart is the center of "the inner mind or feeling nature that transcends the senses" (ibid., pp. 51). Frawley tells us, the nature of our Consciousness is "a product of our deepest relationships"...our associations with others are what really matter (ibid., pp. 79).

Chapter 10

The Other Choice

Whether the problem is a personal matter, in a group, or on a national or international scale, all conflict stems from a threat to our identity and all conflict involves self proving. Zen Master Shunryu Suzuki put it this way, "The cause of conflict is some fixed idea or one-sided idea" (1997, pp. 74). To jar ourselves loose, we use Compassion and Forgiveness. Both help us understand that not everyone sees the world as we do, nor should they...and that we don't know and that's okay. There is one more part to the lesson conflict has to teach us.

Pain and More Pain

We enter in the middle of a lengthy conversation between two co-parents:

Co-Parent 1: "I can't believe you still have no idea how this has affected your family. I just can't get over it–"

Co-Parent 2: "This. This? What is this? You keep talking around it as though it's something real?"

Co-Parent 1: "Please, tell me you're kidding. Your children have suffered beyond what anyone should have to go through. Do you know what we've been through? No, damn it, no, you can't have the kids for overnights because you just won't admit the horrible ordeal they've been through."

Co-Parent 2: "Nothing happened to those kids. You

have cooked this entire thing up in your head... and you've convinced the kids–"

Co-Parent 1: "Your entire family was deposed! And my family and my Mother explained to the police exactly how different the kids have been since that night and she–"

Co-Parent 2: "And my Dad clearly stated that nothing happened. Everyone knows you've conjured this thing up and created this huge story to discredit my family and make sure my reputation is–"

Co-Parent 1: "Your cousin was there. I'm sorry, you can think what you want, but I have evidence that he was there that night at your house. I have documentation that his car–"

Co-Parent 2: "So what? He was there because he works for me. Of course he was there. So what?"

Co-Parent 1: "Don't you care at all? Do you know what your kids have been through?"

Co-Parent 2: "Nothing happened. Nothing. The police interviewed all of us, they found nothing. You've got the kids all worked up. How could you ever think I would allow anything to happen to my kids? How can you think this of me?"

Co-Parent 1: "The kids could not have made this up. The psychologist I took them to said the words they used, the private parts they pointed to, the explanation they gave was too descriptive to be made up. They're children, for God's sake, how can you just sit there?"

Co-Parent 2: "Because nothing happened! You and your parents put these ideas in their heads. You've led them on for more than a year now. They're confused and I don't think they know what's real anymore. The police are comfortable that nothing happened. The court agrees. The psychiatrist I took them to said the kids are suffering from us continuing to fight over this and your inability to let this thing go. You've got to let this go. This is insane!"

Co-Parent 1: "He's got a criminal record!"

Co-Parent 2: "For burglary – what, ten years ago? He was a kid. He's a grown person now. He's a good worker. He's a good person. He would never hurt those kids. And he was at work; he was never alone with the kids. Why are you pressing this?"

Co-Parent 1: "The children have suffered enough. A simple admission from you would help us all get over this. Please, I beg of you, help us heal."

Co-Parent 2: "Nothing happened. I'm sure of it. I beg of you, let this go. You're hurting everyone, especially the kids."

So, who's telling the truth?

The fact is they both are. From each of their vantage points, they are both telling their own truth. As difficult and as painful as it may be to accept in this particular case, there are multiple truths and no fact, no documentation, no proof will ever convince these two co-parents otherwise. Very often, in situations of extreme conflict, there are *multiple* truths. This is especially so in cases of social identity conflict where the conflict spans multiple lifetimes, memories are selective, and the extent of "un-rightable wrongs" can be beyond imagination.

The point is the truth has its limits. Any person involved in criminal investigations knows eyewitness reports are highly unreliable: two people can witness the very same event and see it in entirely different ways. So, too, the court system seldom gets to "the truth" but rather, weighs among multiple versions of it. Similarly, psychological assessments, another tool we'd like to believe is foolproof, "cannot determine who's telling the truth... figure out what happened in the past...determine if a child has been sexually abused...[and] usually can't say which parent is better suited to have custody of a child" (Gaulier, Price, and Windell, 2007, pp. 134-6). There are limits to "the truth".

Individuals and groups of people having wholly different viewpoints on the same topic can *both be right*. A company contract proposal can be both, its best offer and an affront to union members; people sleeping on the street in skid row can be both, a public nuisance and entitled to their civil liberties; religious beliefs can be both, a salvation and consolation to some and the source of history's most horrific atrocities. In science, this is called Complementarity: not opposites but two complementary views of the same reality. In the mediation field, this is a known fact: we can't mediate beliefs or what happened. People will always believe their own truths; no mediation session or negotiation technique will ever change that. Beliefs and truths can be discussed and they should be, but not with the intent of trying to change them or get to "the" truth.

This One I Simply Cannot Buy

To say that both parties can be right, especially in a case like the one presented above, is a difficult pill to swallow. How can children be abused and not abused? Or, in the case of social identity conflict, how can Israel have settlement outposts and not have settlement outposts? It just doesn't wash.

Try another example:

A small town is in an uproar over the influx of illegal aliens into their community. Once a quiet, mixed neighborhood of middle class Black and White citizens, the town is now overrun by Mexicans who hang out in the parking lot all day long, looking for day labor. The town is trying to enact laws to clean up the mess: to make it a crime to hang out in parking lots, to have illegal immigrants arrested, and to limit the number of Mexican immigrants who move into their town. In this latter case, they hope to mirror a law recently enacted that makes it illegal for homeless people to loiter in community parks or malls. The citizens say they just want their community back. They want to feel safe again, and not overrun.

Not all the Mexican immigrants are illegal. They came to this town because friends and family members had moved there and they wanted to feel as "at home" as possible. Some are illegal, yet all are working or looking for work. They claim they came to the United States for the same reason everyone comes; the same reason the Irish, German, and other Europeans once came. They want a good life. They want to protect and educate their children. They want the right to self determination; to decide their own future, be treated in a dignified manner, and be in control of their lives. They argue that America is in transition; that majorities and minorities shift in a democracy. They suggest that no-one owns their community with assurances it will stay a particular way.

So, whose truth is right? Again, they both are. It's *their* truth. From where they sit, they're both right. This is not the same as saying that both "truths" can be realized simultaneously. Yet, it doesn't eliminate that possibility either.

The Third Option

We are in the midst of some pretty tough times and the future promises only to get tougher. The problems we face are more numerous, complex, and interdependent, and conflict itself is growing more narrowly defined. The more intractable the conflict, the greater the likelihood there is multiple truths. In other words, there's *no one right way*. There will always be another point of view, another set of desirable outcomes, and another way of getting there. Moreover, no-one can be "doing the right thing"; we each have our own "right thing" and it may or may not be shared by others. For those of us who have always prided ourselves on having the answer, being a "solver", and knowing the way out, we've got some learning to do. No-one is doing *the* right thing; not now, and even less so in the future. There will always be another way. There will always be a third option.

We find that option through a **Pause**. Whether the problem is an individual matter or social identity conflict, we focus our attention, Notice, and breathe. We adopt a Beginner's Mind and Reflect *first*. We grow present and hear. And then we pause. A pause is full of opportunities. It's the final technique for getting along in tough times; the next step towards greater awareness. We pause without knowing the right answer or needing to do the right thing. We simply pause.

We pause after the conversation has progressed far enough that many of the needs, interests, and emotions have been exposed and discussed. In a pause, we Notice the knee-jerk reaction to institutionally self-prove. We Notice the desire to find something solid; something to hold on to. A pause is a chance to go deeper. It's a chance to see our own biases and confront the unconscious stereotypes we apply everyday, and especially when we feel threatened. It's a time to innovate and contribute to "the competition of ideas." In a pause, we choose how to proceed. We choose how to elevate, examine, and address the fundamental concerns – the issues of image, beliefs, and survival...dignity, recognition, and safety which mean so much. In other words, we stop resisting and let go to what is. In a pause, conflict becomes a process of *mutual exploration and discovery*.

Ask a Good Question and Make a Request

In a pause, we might find the process of mutual exploration and discovery is best served by asking some good questions. Questions are a key tool for exploring value differences and existential needs, and coming to understand them. We might go deeper by asking:

- Why is that?
- How is this important to you?
- What's the history that surrounds that?
- How could I understand this more?
- What would be helpful right now?
- What is it you want me to understand about that?
- What's the cost of us cooperating on this?
- How did you take that, what I just said?
- What is this really about, from where you sit?
- If that weren't the problem, what other explanations might there be?
- What other reasons might explain what happened?
- How do you think that gets played out?
- What does that look like over the long term?
- Has there ever been an exception to that policy/ approach?

Or, depending on where one is in the conversation:
- What would happen if we did nothing?
- What do we need to do to get past the next couple of weeks or months?
- What are the consequences of doing it that way?
- What alternatives have been considered already?
- What options have or haven't worked in the past?
- What would convey our disapproval and still, facilitate a resolution?
- What if this/that fails? What then?

To ask a good question, we might consider _contrasting_. With contrasting, we first present what we _don't_ want. We might say, "What I don't want is for you to feel like I'm interrogating you or trying to make you feel uncomfortable. What I'm wondering is, why you feel that way?" Or, "Perhaps you're right, we'll probably never agree on this, but that doesn't stop us from talking about it, does it?"

Alternatively, in a pause, we might find the process of mutual exploration and discovery is best served by making a request. A request forces us to specify what we want, which requires that we know what we want. Sometimes, and particularly in social identity conflict, we're so busy being angry, we haven't fully formulated what it is we want; or worse, we want "communication", "respect", "dignity", or "self determination" and have no idea what that really means. Making a request also ensures we don't simply present a problem and expect someone else to solve it, which often happens in the workplace. It's our responsibility to take the time we need to understand the problem, and to have some thoughts on how to solve it.

A request helps focus the conversation and begin the task of problem-solving. Yet it is also a key tool for exploring fixed ideas and attachments. Biases and stereotypes are often hidden in our thoughts on how to solve a problem. When we make a request, the request itself becomes part of the process of mutual exploration. We encourage the other person or group to ask questions about our request so our "truths" can be revealed. When a request is made of us, we Reflect _first_ for the very same reason.

A Transpersonal Approach to Conflict

Transpersonal means moving beyond the ego; we expand our awareness to a place beyond an identity and a self. When applied to conflict, it doesn't assume the absence of self interest; rather, self interest is not the _only_ principle that's operating. In a transpersonal approach, we're not looking for the answer or trying to find a middle ground. We are seeking a higher plane.

In a transpersonal view of conflict, we actively engage in the competition of ideas. Ideas are generated through the process of mutual exploration and discovery, by asking smart questions, and through the exchange of mutual requests. Instead of solutions, we incorporate the universal truths of change, impermanence, and groundlessness, and think in terms of decisions, or more precisely, a series of *iterative decisions*. We acknowledge, up-front, that there's always a third option and approach every decision as temporary, a form of trial and error. And while the lengthy process of discovery ensures we take a *longer* horizon into consideration, we accept that nothing is final. Conditions change, and even the best decisions change with time.

Most importantly, a transpersonal approach to conflict *begins with the individual.* We already know that change begets change; once we do something different and interrupt the pattern, future change becomes easier. So, too, it's up to each of us to start the transition: to set an example by putting our egos in check when we deal with differences. We each start the flow and usher in the sea-change. Only through our individual action can we affect how conflict is dealt with across cultures and in the world-at-large.

Iterative Decisions

In the difficult times that lie ahead, some problems will trump others. These are the problems we *create* by our ego-driven behavior. They are so complex and so inter-connected that they will mandate a transpersonal approach to conflict. Global climate change is a case in point. Global climate change – who's to blame and how to fix it – is a social identity conflict in the making. As Al Gore states in his book, An Inconvenient Truth, "Scientists overwhelmingly agree that the Earth is getting warmer, [and] that the trend is caused by people" (2006, pp. 308). Yet the U.S. government remains at odds with many other countries and the scientific community-at-large with respect to how to take action on global climate change. Long before the U.S. government gets around to tackling the crisis, each of us, as individuals, will be forced to decide how to proceed.

In part, the conflict over global warming is about the extent to which our lifestyle as Americans is responsible for warming the planet. We can begin by asking some good questions and making some requests *of ourselves*. We must explore the contradictions in our own behavior; how we believe natural resources are finite and act as though they aren't. We need to study our own biases and consider whether we feel entitled to be wasteful or put ourselves first. We must question whether "we've gone straight from denial to despair" (ibid., pp. 276), accepting the inevitability of the crisis and grabbing what we can in the meantime.

In particular, we need to examine how attached we are to the specifics of how we live. Every time we turn on the AC at the slightest inkling of discomfort, let the car idle to keep it warm while we run inside to make a purchase, buy something we don't need, or throw away a water bottle/styrofoam cup/unused napkin, we need to Notice and breathe deeply, and Reflect *first*. And then, we Pause: to explore and discover our part in this problem, the beliefs and values that sustain it, and to decide how to proceed. We act by taking a series of personal, iterative decisions. We ask ourselves, "Okay, we've done the obvious: changed to compact fluorescent lights, committed to run only full loads of wash, use a clothesline instead of the dryer. What next?" Can we:
- Turn the lights off when we leave the room?
- Turn the water off when we're brushing our teeth?
- Close off certain rooms when we're running the

AC or heat?
- Car pool, consolidate trips, or limit driving altogether?
- Move the dryer away from the freezer, or oven away from the frig?
- Turn off the appliances we're not using?
- Buy local, and measure the carbon miles of our food?
- Invest our money in greener industries?

And after that, what then? Can we:
- Partially dry our hair before using the blow dryer?
- Use a reusable mug for our morning coffee?
- Purchase re-usable bags to avoid paper and plastic altogether?
- Eliminate all duplicate magazines or those we don't want/use?
- Use power strips or unplug the TV, chargers, DVD players, and anything with a remote?

And after that, what then? Can we:
- Use non-toxic alternatives to chemical cleaners?
- Set our hot water temperature to 120 degrees Fahrenheit?
- Drive at 55 miles per hour?
- Use reusable bottles for water, soda, and juice?
- Use organic lawn fertilizers?
- Drive a well-tuned car at all times?

And after that, what then? What can we *give up*?
- Do we need to take all those napkins? Or use all that toilet paper?
- Do we need a stirrer for every cup of coffee?

- Can we pre-cycle by not buying in the first place?
- Can we avoid the fads: the elaborate house decorations and light displays, the leave blowers, the walkway sweepers?
- Can we do without our disposable clothing? The new T-shirt which takes, on average, 1 lb. of pesticides to produce?
- Can we eliminate paper towels?
- Can we stop using twist-ties and other items that can't be recycled?
- Can we think about how things are packaged before we buy? Whether the packaging is excessive and/or re-cyclable?
- Can we buy less for the holidays, do away with wrapping paper and non-degradable tinsel, and consider a re-usable tree?
- Can we consider donations instead of wedding presents and birthday gifts?
- Can we begin to factor in the planetary costs of goods and services?

Can we give up some of our nuttier habits, such as taking a hot shower with the AC running, eating hot food in the summer and then cooling down with bottled water, or standing with the refrigerator door open and starring into it? The question is, just how far can we go? A collection of individual iterative decisions that set an example for others, can quickly add up to a planet-sized solution.

The Final Key

When differences are approached as a process of mutual exploration and discovery, we reach for a higher plane – where we connect with others, create a marketplace of ideas, and take action *consciously*. To attain this place, we are forever **Opening**, which is the third and final key to getting along in tough times. Opening unlocks our attachment to one right way.

In science, there are special systems that deliberately stay off balance as a way to ensure they continue to grow and innovate. Dissipative structures, for example, use change to create a new form that is better suited to the environment (Wheatley, 1994, pp. 19). In dissipative structures that involve chemical reactions, "entropy has increased but...as long as the system stays open to the environment...the system will avoid equilibrium and remain... 'exquisitely ordered'" (ibid., pp. 89). In some Eastern traditions as well, the goal is not equilibrium but a continuous process of rest, change, and a resultant new level of diversification. In Ayurveda, these stages are known as Tamas or dullness/inertia, Rajas or change/energy, and Sattwa or clarity/light. Change always involves action and some level of pain, and yet to remain the same, involves more pain.

Opening is critical for innovation and change. It allows us to counteract inertia and reach for Sattwa. That's what NASA did when it initiated an on-line contest for innovative ideas, such as more flexible gloves for astronauts. Other companies are doing it too, through "crowd sourcing" by inviting "non-experts" to contribute their ideas and inventions. Crowd sourcing is an example of "Beginner's Mind" in action. In a conflict situation, we are forever Opening to the many different ways innovation can occur: the strange bedfellows we keep, the odd ideas we entertain, the unusual people we meet along the way. We use ideas and change to keep ourselves a little off balance; so we don't succumb to the natural process of contraction, we open.

A transpersonal approach to conflict is a continuous process of Opening. We open to the many ways of perceiving reality, the numerous places we get stuck along the way, and the possibility and potential of different truths and multiple "right ways". We open to the plethora of plausible outcomes and the many ways of getting there. We open to the belief that together, the answers are there to be found, and to the prospect of moving on. Finally, we open to a new level of awareness...beyond "me" and "you", and even "us"... beyond the ego, an identity, and a self...to a new place where there's nothing to prove.

A Transpersonal Approach
to Dealing with Differences

The lesson conflict has to teach us is the potential of moving beyond the ego. The Transpersonal approach applies to individual conflict, conflict within and among groups, and conflict on the world stage. The same principles apply:

(1) Differences are normal, they should be expected.

(2) Without awareness, we naturally contract.

(3) With contraction, we engage in three mental lockdowns: we assume everyone sees the world as we do, we assume we know, and we assume there's one right way.

(4) All behavior is a choice. Absent awareness, it's a habit, a form of contraction, and habits are very hard to break.

(5) All behavior is functional. It makes sense, even if we don't understand it.

(6) All conflict involves a threat to our identity and we re-act to that threat by self proving.

(7) Change begets change. After the first change, future change becomes easier.

(8) Relationships are more important than problems and worth preserving. Differences need to be explored and understood.

(9) The more intractable conflict becomes, the greater the likelihood of multiple truths.

(10) It is better to try something different than a tried-and-true, habitual approach; to not know, than to know; and to make iterative decisions, than to find the solution.

A Transpersonal approach to conflict relies on three primary techniques: Noticing, Reflecting *first*, and Pausing. In using these techniques, we learn to be present, to help without doing, and to adopt a Beginner's Mind. Ultimately, they lead to the three keys for getting along: Compassion, Forgiveness, and Opening. Together, these form the people skills we need for dealing with differences in tough times. The task ahead depends on each of us: to move beyond "me" and "you", and even "us".

Bibliography

Ajaya, Swami. *Psychotherapy East and West.* Honesdale, PA: Himalayan Institute, 1983.

Anselmo, P., and Brooks, J. *Ayurvedic Secrets to Longevity and Total Health.* Englewood Cliffs, New Jersey: Prentice Hall, 1996.

Benson, H., and Stuart, E. *The Wellness Book.* New York: Fireside, 1992.

Bolton, R. *People Skills: How to Assert Yourself, Listen to Others and Settle Disputes.* New York: Simon and Schuster, Inc., 1979.

Burgess, H., and Burgess, G. "Intractability and the Frontier of the Field." *Conflict Resolution Quarterly,* Volume 24, Number 2, Winter, 2006.

Bush, R., and Folger, J. *The Promise of Mediation: The Transformative Approach to Conflict,* 2d ed. San Francisco: Jossey-Bass, 2005.

Chopra, D. *The Book of Secrets: Unlocking the Hidden Dimensions of Your Life.* New York: Three Rivers Press, 2004.

Collins, J. *Good to Great.* New York: HarperCollins, 2001.

Davis, L. *I Thought We'd Never Speak Again.* New York: First Quill, 2003.

Douillard, J. *Body, Mind and Sport.* New York: Crown Trade Paperbacks, 1994.

Dozier, R. *Why We Hate: Understanding, Curbing, and Eliminating Hate in Ourselves and Our World.* New York: McGraw-Hill, 2002.

Easwaran, E. *Dialogue with Death: A Journey Through Consciousness,* 2d ed. Berkeley, CA: Nilgiri Press, 1992.

Epstein, M. *Thoughts Without a Thinker.* New York: Basic Books, 1995.

Fahri, D. *The Breathing Book.* New York: Henry Holt and Company, 1996.

Feuerstein, G. *The Yoga Tradition: Its History, Literature, Philosophy and Practice.* Prescott, AZ: Hohm Press, 2001.

_____. *The Shambala Guide to Yoga.* Boston: Shambala Publications, 1996.

Feuerstein, G., and Bodian, S. *Living Yoga: A Comprehensive Guide for Daily Life.* New York: Tarcher/Putnam Books, 1993.

Firman, J., and Gila, A. *The Primal Wound.* Albany, New York: SUNY, 1997.

Fisher, R., Kopelman, E., and Kupper-Schneider, A. *Beyond Machiavelli: Tools for Coping with Conflict.* New York: Penguin Books, 1996.

Fisher, R., and Ury, W. *Getting to Yes: Negotiating Agreement Without Giving In.* Boston: Houghton Mifflin, 1981.

Folger, J., Scott Poole, M., Stutman, R. *Working Through Conflict: Strategies for Relationships, Groups, and Organizations,* 5th ed. Boston: Peason Education, Inc., 2005.

Frawley, D. *Ayurveda and The Mind, The Healing of Consciousness.* Twin Lakes, WI: Lotus Press, 1996.

_____. *From the River of Heaven.* Salt Lake City, Utah: Passage Press, 1990.

Gaulier, B., Margerum, J., Price, J., and Windell, J. *DeFusing the High-Conflict Divorce: A Treatment Guide for Working with Angry Couples.* Atascadero, CA: Impact Publishers, 2007.

Gaussen, T. "The Development of Personhood and the Brain" in Watson, G., Batchelor, S., and Claxton, G (eds.), *The Psychology of Awakening: Buddhism, Science, and Our Day-to-Day Lives.* York Beach, Maine: Samuel Weiser, Inc., 2000.

Gladwell, M. *Blink.* New York: Little, Brown, and Company, 2005.

Goleman, D. *Social Intelligence: The New Science of Human Relationships.* New York: Bantam Books, 2006.

_____. *Emotional Intelligence: Why It Can Matter More Than IQ,* 10th Anniversary Reissue ed. New York: Bantam Deli,

2006.

Goleman, D., and Gurin, J. (eds.) *Mind-Body Medicine: How to Use Your Mind for Better Health.* Yonder, NY: Consumer Reports Books, 1993.

Gore, A. *An Inconvenient Truth.* New York: Melcher Media, 2006.

Kabat-Zin, J. *Full Catastrophe Living.* New York: Delta, 1990.

Keller, D. *Refining the Breath: Pranayama in the Anusara Style of Yoga,* 2d ed. South Riding, VA: Do Yoga Productions, 2001.

Knaster, M. *Discovering the Body's Wisdom.* New York: Bantam New Age, 1996.

Kolb, D., and Williams, J. *Everyday Negotiations: Navigating the Hidden Agendas In Bargaining.* San Francisco: Jossey-Bass, 2003.

Kottler, J., *Beyond Blame: A New Way of Resolving Conflicts in Relationships.* San Francisco: Jossey-Bass, 1994.

Kressel, K. "The Strategic Style in Mediation." *Conflict Resolution Quarterly,* Volume 24, Number 3, Spring 2007.

Lad, V. *Ayurveda: The Science of Self Healing.* Wilmot, WI: Lotus Press, 1984.

LeBaron, M. *Bridging Troubled Waters: Conflict Resolution From The Heart.* San Francisco: Jossey-Bass, 2002.

Leifer, R. *The Happiness Project: Transforming the Three Poisons that Cause the Suffering We Inflict on Ourselves and Others.* Ithaca, New York: Snow Lion Publications, 1997.

Lieven, A., and Hulsman, J. *Ethical Realism, A Vision for America's Role in the World.* New York: Pantheon Books, 2006.

Maiese, M. "Engaging the Emotions in Conflict Intervention." *Conflict Resolution Quarterly,* Volume 24, Number 2, Winter 2006.

Moore, C. W. *The Mediation Process: Practical Strategies for Resolving Conflict,* 3d ed. San Francisco: Jossey-Bass, 2003.

Morrison, J. *The Book of Ayurveda.* New York: Fireside, 1995.

Muni, Swami R. *Yoga: The Ultimate Spiritual Path*, 2d ed. St. Paul, MN: Llewellyn Publications, 2001.

Nelson, J. "Madness or Transcendence, Looking to the Ancient East for a Modern Transpersonal Diagnostic System" in Seymour Boorstein (ed), *Transpersonal Psychotherapy*, 2d ed. Albany, New York: SUNY Press, 1996.

Notarius, C., and Markman, H. *We Can Work It Out.* New York: The Berkeley Publishing Group, 1993.

Oren, M. *Power, Faith, and Fantasy.* New York: W.W. Norton & Co., 2007.

Orstein, R., and Sobel, D. *The Healing Brain.* Cambridge, MA: Malor Books, 1999.

Patterson, K., Grenny, J., McMillan, R., and Switzler, A. *Crucial Conversations.* New York: McGraw-Hill, 2005.

Richmond, L. *Work as a Spiritual Practice.* New York: Broadway Books, 1999.

Rosenberg, M. *Nonviolent Communication: A Language of Life.* Encinitas, CA: Puddle Dancer Press, 2003.

Rothman, J. *Resolving Identity-Based Conflict in Nations, Organizations, and Communities.* San Francisco: Jossey-Bass, 1997.

Shantananda, Swami, and Bendet, P. *The Splendor of Recognition.* South Fallsburg, New York: SYDA Foundation, 2003.

Shmueli, D., Elliot, M., and Kaufman, S. "Frame Changes and the Management of Intractable Conflicts." *Conflict Resolution Quarterly*, Volume 24, Number 2, Winter, 2006.

Sills, M. "Licking Honey from the Razor's Edge" in Watson, G., Batchelor, S., and Claxton, G. (eds.), *The Psychology of Awakening: Buddhism, Science, and Our Day-to-Day Lives.* York Beach, Maine: Samuel Weiser, Inc., 2000.

Stone, D., Patton, B., and Heen, S. *Difficult Conversations.* New York: Penguin Books, 1999.

Stryker, R. "Maha Mudra." *Yoga Journal*, March-April, 2007.

Suzuki, S. *Zen Mind, Beginner's Mind*, 37th Printing. New York: Weatherhill, Inc., 1997.

Tolle, E. *The Power of Now: A Guide to Spiritual Enlightenment.* Novato, CA: New World Library, 1999.

Tomlinson, E., and Lewicki, R. "Managing Distrust In Intractable Conflicts." *Conflict Resolution Quarterly,* Volume 24, Number 2, Winter 2006.

Varela, F. "Steps to a Science of Inter-Being: Unfolding the Dharma Implicity in Modern Cognitive Science" in Watson, G., Batchelor, S., and Claxton, G (eds.), *The Psychology of Awakening: Buddhism, Science, and Our Day-to-Day Lives.* York Beach, Maine: Samuel Weiser, Inc., 2000.

Wheatley, M. *Leadership and the New Science: Learning about Organization from an Orderly Universe.* San Francisco: Berret Koehler Publishers, 1992.

Welwood, J. *Toward A Psychology of Awakening: Buddhism, Psychotherapy, and the Path of Personal and Spiritual Transformation.* Boston: Shambala Publications, 2000.

Subject Index

A

Active Listening: as a basic tool, 28-29; as compared to Reflect first, 91-92
Albany Times Union, 138
Association for Conflict Resolution, 6
Assumptions: in general, 52; assuming we know, 73, 81-83
Automatic Pilot, 18, 53, 68, 135
Awareness: being present, 110-111; Noticing and, 63-64; Reflect first and, 95; Opening and, 155-156; lesson of conflict, 9-10
Ayurveda: body types, 96-97; general description of, 96; personalized program of, 110-112; mind and, 142-143; work and, 119

B

Beginner's Mind, 90, 107-108, 156
Body Armor, 62
Body Types: general description of, 96-97; effect of work on, 119
Brain: limbic, 60, 139; stress and, 60
Breathing, 64-65

C

Chakras, 57-58
Change: as a constant, 140; begetting change, 68; other party needing to, 83-84
Choice, 24, 68, 128-129
Compassion, 68-69, 84, 120, 127
Conflict: as individuals, groups, and on world stage, 4-6; at work, 113-118; awareness and, 10; hate and, 138-140; process of mutual exploration and discovery, 148-149; styles of 87-88; tactics and strategies in, 115-116; transpersonal approach to, 151-152
Conflict Escalation: in general, 32-34; personal role in, 40
Conflict Resolution: in the US Navy, 31-32; styles of, 20-24, 34-38. See Also Interests-based, Strategic, and Transformative.
Consciousness: conditioning and, 52; ego-based, 57-58; higher levels of, 142-143; process of contraction and, 84-85
Contrasting, 151
Crowd Sourcing, 156

D

Disempowered Parent, 95
Dissipative Structures, 156

E

Ego: chakra, 57-58; ego-based consciousness, 57-58; preya and, 128-129; role in self, 51; social identity conflict and, 135-136
Emotional Intelligence, 60
Emotions: at work, 117; handling emotions in mediation, 37-38; labeling emotions and feelings, 88-89; stress and, 60-62
Energy: as an organizing principle, 57;contraction and, 84-85; becoming physical, 69; energy types and energetic imprint, 96-97

F

Feelings: naming, 88-89; unaddressed, 102; work and, 117
Fixers, 82
Forgiveness, 95, 120, 127
Fractals, 70
Framing: at work, 116-117; general description of, 75-77
Functional Behavior, 95

G

Gadgetry, 118
Global Warming, 152-155
Groundlessness, 141
Groups, 114-115
Group Think, 114

H

Hate, 138-140
Hearing, 90-91
Help: new definition of, 98-99
Humor, 107

I

Identity: general description of, 48-49; threat to and conflict, 54-56; social identity, 133-135; universal contraction and, 84-85
Imbalances, 118-119
Impermanence, 140
Interests-Based Negotiations: general description of, 34-36; handling emotions in, 38; social identity conflict and, 138
Institutionalized Self Proving, 136-138
Interactive Decisions, 152-155

K

Kali-Yuga, 41
Kashmir Shaivism, 57, 84-85
Keys: Compassion, 68-69, Forgiveness, 95; Opening, 155-156

M

Mediation: books on, 7-8; interests-based negotiations, 34-36; handling emotions in, 37-38; in general 6-7; mediating beliefs, 147; strategic style, 36; transformative style, 37-39
Mental Locks: description of, 53-54; first, 54; second, 78, 81-83; third, 135-138
Middle East, 133, 135, 141-142

M (CONT.)

Mind: assumptions and, 52; contraction of, 52-53; Don't Know Mind, 90; interconnected mind, 142-143; mind-reading, 82; quieting the, 110-112; in self development, 51-53

Mind Ruts: description of, 52; frames and, 75-77; national 141-142

Mirror Neurons, 75

Moral Imperative, 137-138

N

Narrowcasting, 115

NASA, 156

National Public Radio, 137

Noticing: as compared to self awareness, 63-64; in general 62-63; in reltion to hearing, 90

O

One Right Way, 135-136

P

Pause, 149-151

People Skills, by Richard Bolton, 9

Positional Bargaining: as a reaction, 55; at work, 115; compared to Interests-based, 35; description of 20-24; in social identity conflict, 138

Positive Language, 26-27

Prana, 65

Preya and Shreya, 128-129

Present: awareness and, 84-85; at work, 125; in a conversation, 98,110-112

Primary Fears, 51

P (CONT.)

Problem Solving, 2-3, 151

Psychological Assessments, 146-147

Puranas, 41

Q

Questions, 126-127, 150

R

Reactions: as compared to responses, 68; in general, 53; interrupting the pattern of, 62-63; positional bargaining as, 22; to another's self proving, 86

Reading People, 73-75

Reflect first: description of, 92-94; in a conversation, 104-106; to crystallize issues, 108-109

Reframing, 108

Relationships: preserving, 126-127;styles of conflict in, 87-88; work and, 116. See also Section Three.

Requests, 149-151

Resistance, 49, 60, 140-141,149

Role of Management, 125-127

S

Secret Struggle, 102-103

Self: as I-centered, 51; as real, 53-54; conflict as a threat to, 54-56; development of, 49-51

Self Awareness, 63-64

Self Proving: as a reaction to conflict, 49, 54-56; as in the way of resolving conflict, 59; institutionalized, 136-138; stress and, 60; work and, 113

S (CONT.)

Shadow Negotiations, 83
Shreya and Preya, 128-129
Silence, 107
Social Identity Conflict: as a mind rut,141; definition of, 133-134; examples of, 133; third mental lock and, 135. See Also Chapter Nine.
Social Intelligence, 74-75
Spindle Cells, 75
Stereotypes: as an assumption, 52; hate and, 139
Strategic Style of Negotiation, 36
Stress, 60-62, 118-119

T

Tantra, 57
Tangential Issues, 83, 102
Therapizing, 82, 102
Threatened: as a feeling, 3; fight or flight response, 60; role in conflict, 54-55
Tools: in mediation books, 7-8; problem with, 31; life changing 24-30
Transformative Mediation: and emotions, 37-38; description of, 37-38; Don't Know Mind and, 90; hallmark of, 98
Transparency, 27-28, 108, 123
Transpersonal Approach to Conflict: general description of, 10, 39-40, 151-152
Truth: multiple, 146-147; universal, 140-141

U

Underlying Intelligence, 69-70
Universal Contraction, 84-85
Universal Truths, 140-141
US Navy, 31-32

V

Values, 134

W

Witness, 64
Work: as compared to family conflict, 114-117; forgiveness and, 127. See also Chapter 8.

Y

Yoga: as a Eastern Tradition, 57, 69; being present and, 128; hatha, 41